The Priest

A Bridge to God

The Priest

A Bridge to God

INSPIRATION AND
ENCOURAGEMENT FOR PRIESTS
AND SEMINARIANS

POPE BENEDICT XVI

Selected and Edited by Christopher Bailey

Our Sunday Visitor Publishing Division
Our Sunday Visitor, Inc.
Huntington, IN 46750

ISBN: 978-1-59276-248-4 (Inventory No. T1195)
eISBN: 978-1-61278-212-6
LCCN: 2012932027

Interior design by M. Urgo
Cover design by Rebecca J. Heaston
Cover photo by Stefano Spaziani

PRINTED IN THE UNITED STATES OF AMERICA

CONTENTS

Three / The Priority of Prayer   *43*

Four / Living in the Body of Christ   *57*

FOREWORD

We call him — Pope Benedict XVI — our *Pontiff*, from the Latin word *Pontifex*, which means "bridge builder." The bishop of Rome, the Successor of Saint Peter, the "Servant of the Servants of God," the visible shepherd of the Church Universal, has as his "job description" the building of a bridge between the Creator and His creatures.

A rather awesome and intimidating portfolio! This "bridge building" has of course already been done, with infinite efficacy, by the One whose cross that afternoon we strangely call "good" carried us *across* the bridge from earth to heaven, from sin to grace, from death to life. Jesus is *the* Pontiff; we really need no other — except to reflect and remind us of Jesus. The Master was a shrewd teacher, the best educational psychologist ever, and he knew he would need reminders, signs, "sacraments" here on this side of the bridge to hint at the other side.

One such sign is the one whom we Catholics sometimes call the *Sovereign Pontiff*, our Holy Father.

Lord knows that he has surely been a very effective vicar of the essential "bridge builder," the carpenter's son from Nazareth. In his words, writings, teachings, travels, and gentle presence, Pope Benedict XVI has helped us "bridge the gap" between Creator and creature.

Now he offers us priests and future priests the high compliment of calling us "bridges" as well.

Blessed John Paul II, in his renowned exhortation on priestly formation, *Pastores Dabo Vobis*, reminded priests and seminarians that our personality, our humanity, our temperament can either bring people closer to God and His Church or drive them away.

In other words, we can be a *bridge*, or a wall.

"My beloved priests," Pope Benedict exhorts, "tear down this wall!"

Let your ministry, your own nature, your very personality, remind people of the tender, gentle, loving mercy of Jesus!

Thank you, Our Sunday Visitor. A hundred years after that great priest and bishop, John Francis Noll, founded this providential publishing endeavor, you continue to "feed the sheep."

And, in this elegant and timely book, you feed the shepherds as well.

✠ *Timothy Cardinal Dolan*
Archbishop of New York
February 22, 2012
Feast of the Chair of St. Peter

ONE

IT DOES MAKE SENSE

It does make sense to become a priest," Pope Benedict XVI assures us. That's sometimes hard to remember when it seems like the whole world is telling you that it doesn't make sense. Our secular culture laughs at priests — or, even worse, fears and denounces them. At best, it dismisses them as rather old-fashioned. Is there really any room in the modern world for the priesthood?

The Holy Father has a startling answer for the naysayers. We need priests now more than ever, he says. It's not the priesthood that's passing away, but the secular culture. The priest is the man of the future. When every memory of modern popular culture has passed away, the priesthood will endure.

Joseph Ratzinger grew up in Nazi Germany under a regime that was fanatically hostile to Catholic Christianity. Over and over he was told that his silly notion of becoming a priest was absurd, useless, outdated, impossible. There would be no priests in the perfect new world of National Socialism.

Yet the Catholic Church is still here, whereas the Nazis have been swept into the dustbin. His long life has given the Holy Father an important historical perspective. He has watched first-hand as the dominant secular philosophies of the twentieth century — fascism and communism — have been swept away, while the Catholic Church has remained the dominant force in the world's thought.

There will be times when reading what Pope Benedict has to say takes a little bit of work. When the Holy Father speaks, he does not water down the truth. He trusts us to be able to understand anything he understands if we put our minds to it. And you'll find that his trust is seldom misplaced, because he expresses complex ideas precisely and clearly.

But more often we hear a voice that's surprisingly down-to-earth. He knows what his fellow priests are going through — he's gone through it, too, and probably worse. He knows what works for a priest: what encourages him, what motivates him, what keeps him going when it's all too tempting to give up.

And that's the encouragement every priest and seminarian needs. It *does* make sense to become a priest, because the priest is the man of the future. "And the world passes away, and the lust of it; but he who does the will of God abides for ever" (1 John 2:17).

Reverend Kenneth Barclay
904 – 120 Donald Street
Winnipeg, MB R3C 4G2

I was drafted for military service, the
...sked each of us what we planned to do
... I wanted to become a Catholic priest.
... you ought to look for something else. In
... no longer needed." I knew that this "new
... g to an end, and that, after the enormous
... d brought upon the country, priests would
... oday the situation is completely changed. In
... y people nowadays also think that the Cath-
... " for the future, but one that belongs more
... ds, have decided to enter the seminary and
... istry in the Catholic Church in spite of such
... You have done a good thing. Because people
... God, even in an age marked by technical mas-
... obalization: they will always need the God who
... Jesus Christ, the God who gathers us together in
... in order to learn with him and through him life's
true ... order to uphold and apply the standards of true
humanity ... God ... alive, and he needs people to serve him and bring
him to others. It does make sense to become a priest: the world needs
priests, pastors, today, tomorrow, and always, until the end of time.

— *Letter to Seminarians, October 18, 2010*

To **think about:** Why did I want to become a priest? How am I
living that desire — that vocation — in my ministry now?

AIDS ON THE JOURNEY

I grew up in a world very different from the world today, but in the end situations are similar.

On the one hand, the situation of "Christianity" still existed, where it was normal to go to church and to accept the faith as the revelation of God, and to try to live in accordance with his revelation; on the other, there was the Nazi regime, which loudly stated: "In the new Germany there will be no more priests, look for another career." However, it was precisely in hearing these "loud" voices, that I realized that there was instead a great need for priests.

This contrast, the sight of that anti-human culture, confirmed my conviction that the Lord, the Gospel, and the faith were pointing out the right path, and that we were bound to commit ourselves to ensuring that this path survives. In this situation, my vocation to the priesthood grew with me, almost naturally, without any dramatic events of conversion.

Two other things also helped me on this journey: already as a boy, helped by my parents and by the parish priest, I had discovered the beauty of the Liturgy, and I came to love it more and more because I felt that divine beauty appears in it and that Heaven unfolds before us.

The second element was the discovery of the beauty of knowledge, of knowing God and Sacred Scripture, thanks to which it is possible to enter into that great adventure of dialogue with God that is theology.

— *Encounter with the Youth of the Diocese of Rome,*
St. Peter's Square, April 6, 2006

To think about: How do I keep the beauty of the liturgy before my eyes every time I experience it? Am I tempted just to go through the motions? Does my own part in the liturgy make its beauty visible?

*T*oday too people feel in need of priests who witness to God's infinite mercy with a life totally "conquered" by Christ and who learn to do this in the years of their seminary training. After the Synod in 1990 Pope John Paul II published the Apostolic Exhortation *Pastores Dabo Vobis* in which he returned to and updated the norms of the Council of Trent and stressed above all the necessary continuity between the priest's initial and continuing formation. For him this is a true starting point for an authentic reform of the life and apostolate of priests. It is also the key to preventing the "new evangelization" from being merely an attractive slogan and to ensuring that it is expressed in reality. The foundations laid in seminary formation constitute that indispensable "*humus spirituale*" in which "to learn Christ," letting oneself be gradually configured to him, the one and only High Priest and Good Shepherd. The seminary period should therefore be seen as the actualization of the moment when the Lord Jesus, after calling the Apostles and before sending them out to preach, asks them to be with him (cf. Mk 3:14). When St. Mark recounts the calling of the Twelve Apostles he says that Jesus had a twofold purpose: firstly that they should be with him, and secondly, that they should be sent out to preach. Yet, in being with him always, they really proclaim Christ and bring the reality of the Gospel to the world.

— *General Audience, August 19, 2009*

To think about: What will I carry with me for the rest of my life from my seminary formation?

IF YOU LOVE ME ...

*I*f you love me." Dear friends, Jesus said these words at the Last Supper in the context of the moment when he instituted the Eucharist and the priesthood. Although they were addressed to the Apostles, in a certain sense they are addressed to all their successors and to priests who are the closest collaborators of the successors of the Apostles. Let us hear them again today as an invitation to live our vocation in the Church ever more coherently: you, dear Ordinands, listen to them with special emotion because precisely today Christ makes you share in his priesthood. Accept them with faith and with love! Let them be imprinted on your hearts, let them accompany you on the journey of your whole life. Do not forget them; do not lose them on the way! Reread them, meditate on them often, and, especially, pray on them. Thus you will remain faithful to Christ's love and realize with joy ever new that his divine word "walks" with you and "grows" within you.

— *Homily, Ordination of New Priests for the Diocese of Rome,*
St. Peter's Basilica, April 27, 2008

TO THINK ABOUT: Can the people around me see my love for Christ in the way I follow his instructions?

THE SEMINARY MUST BE DEMANDING

*T*he formation offered by the Seminary is demanding, because a portion of the People of God will be entrusted to the pastoral solicitude of the future priests, the People that Christ saved and for whom he gave his life. It is right for seminarians to remember that if the Church demands much of them it is because they are to care for those whom Christ ransomed at such a high price. Many qualities are required of future priests: human maturity, spiritual qualities, apostolic zeal, intellectual rigor....

To achieve these virtues, candidates to the priesthood must not only be able to witness to them to their formation teachers but even more, they must be the first to benefit from these same qualities lived and shared by those who are in charge of helping them to attain maturity. It is a law of our humanity and our faith that we are all too often capable of giving only what we ourselves have previously received from God through the ecclesial and human mediation that he has established. Those who are placed in charge of discernment and formation must remember that the hope they have for others is in the first place a duty for themselves.

— Address to the Community of the French Seminary in Rome,
Clementine Hall, June 6, 2009

TO THINK ABOUT: What was the most difficult thing about the seminary for me? How will that experience inform the rest of my life as a priest?

LOVE IS WHAT COUNTS

Gathered here at Saint Joseph Seminary, I greet the seminarians present and indeed encourage all seminarians throughout America. I am glad to know that your numbers are increasing! The People of God look to you to be holy priests, on a daily journey of conversion, inspiring in others the desire to enter more deeply into the ecclesial life of believers. I urge you to deepen your friendship with Jesus the Good Shepherd. Talk heart to heart with him. Reject any temptation to ostentation, careerism, or conceit. Strive for a pattern of life truly marked by charity, chastity, and humility, in imitation of Christ, the Eternal High Priest, of whom you are to become living icons (cf. *Pastores Dabo Vobis, n.* 33). Dear seminarians, I pray for you daily. Remember that what counts before the Lord is to dwell in his love and to make his love shine forth for others.

— Address, Meeting with Young People and Seminarians,
St. Joseph Seminary, Yonkers, New York, April 19, 2008

TO THINK ABOUT: When I think about my own future, how much of what I'm planning is out of love for Christ, and how much has to do with my own desires?

Becoming truly myself

*H*ere, once more, I think of my own youth. I was somehow aware quite early on that the Lord wanted me to be a priest. Then later, after the war, when I was in the seminary and at university on the way towards that goal, I had to recapture that certainty. I had to ask myself: is this really the path I was meant to take? Is this really God's will for me? Will I be able to remain faithful to him and completely at his service? A decision like this demands a certain struggle. It cannot be otherwise. But then came the certainty: this is the right thing! Yes, the Lord wants me, and he will give me strength. If I listen to him and walk with him, I become truly myself. What counts is not the fulfillment of my desires, but of his will. In this way life becomes authentic.

— Message for the 26th World Youth Day,
August 6, 2010

To think about: How certain do I feel about my future? Am I listening to the Lord and walking with him?

GOD KNOWS HOW TO GIVE YOU JOY

*T*he sadness experienced by the rich young man in the Gospel story is the sadness that arises in the heart of all those who lack the courage to follow Christ and to make the right choice. Yet it is never too late to respond to him!

Jesus never tires of turning to us with love and calling us to be his disciples; to some, however, he proposes an even more radical choice. In this Year for Priests, I would like to urge young men and boys to consider if the Lord is inviting them to a greater gift, along the path of priestly ministry. I ask them to be willing to embrace with generosity and enthusiasm this sign of a special love and to embark on the necessary path of discernment with the help of a priest or a spiritual director. Do not be afraid, then, dear young men and women, if the Lord is calling you to the religious, monastic or missionary life, or a life of special consecration: He knows how to bestow deep joy upon those who respond to him with courage!

— Message on the Occasion of the 25th World Youth Day (March 28, 2010)

TO THINK ABOUT: Does fear for the future keep me from the joy the Lord wants to give me?

FOLLOWING THE STAR

*T*his evangelical passage of the Wise Men who search out and find Jesus has a special meaning precisely for you, dear seminarians, because you are on an authentic journey, engaged in and confirming your call to the priesthood. Why did the Magi set off from afar to go to Bethlehem? The answer has to do with the mystery of the "star" that they saw "in the East" and that they recognized as the sign of the birth of the Messiah (cf. Mt 2:2). So their journey was inspired by a powerful hope, strengthened and guided by the star, which led them towards the King of the Jews, towards the kingship of God himself. This is the meaning behind our journey: to serve the kingship of God in the world.

The Magi set out because of a deep desire that prompted them to leave everything and begin a journey. It was as though they had always been waiting for that star. Dear friends, this is the mystery of God's call, the mystery of vocation. It is part of the life of every Christian, but it is particularly evident in those whom Christ asks to leave everything in order to follow him more closely.

The seminarian experiences the beauty of that call in a moment of grace that could be defined as "falling in love." His soul is filled with amazement, which makes him ask in prayer: "Lord, why me?" But love knows no "why"; it is a free gift to which one responds with the gift of self.

— Address, Meeting with Seminarians, Cologne, August 19, 2005

To think about: What prompted me to begin my journey? Am I still following that star, or have I lost the way?

Study is indispensable

*T*he seminary years are devoted to formation and discernment. Formation, as you well know, has different strands that converge in the unity of the person: it includes human, spiritual, and cultural dimensions. Its deepest goal is to bring the student to an intimate knowledge of the God who has revealed his face in Jesus Christ.

For this, in-depth study of Sacred Scripture is needed, and also of the faith and life of the Church in which the Scripture dwells as the Word of life. This must all be linked with the questions prompted by our reason and with the broader context of modern life.

Such study can at times seem arduous, but it is an indispensable part of our encounter with Christ and our vocation to proclaim him. All this is aimed at shaping a steady and balanced personality, one capable of receiving validly and fulfilling responsibly the priestly mission.

The role of formators is decisive: the quality of the presbyterate in a particular Church depends greatly on that of the seminary, and consequently on the quality of those responsible for formation.

Dear seminarians, for this very reason we pray today with genuine gratitude for your superiors, professors, and educators, who are spiritually present at this meeting. Let us ask the Lord to help them carry out as well as possible the important task entrusted to them.

— *Address, Meeting with Seminarians, Cologne, August 19, 2005*

To think about: How well do I really know the Scriptures? Could I use more in-depth study?

SPRINGTIME IN THE SEMINARY

*T*he seminary years are a time of journeying, of exploration, but above all of discovering Christ. It is only when a young man has had a personal experience of Christ that he can truly understand the Lord's will and consequently his own vocation.

The better you know Jesus the more his mystery attracts you. The more you discover him, the more you are moved to seek him. This is a movement of the Spirit that lasts throughout life, and that makes the seminary a time of immense promise, a true "springtime."

— *Address, Meeting with Seminarians, Cologne, August 19, 2005*

To think about: Am I still discovering Jesus?

MARY INTRODUCES HER SON

*W*hen the Magi came to Bethlehem, "going into the house they saw the child with Mary his mother, and they fell down and worshiped him" (Mt 2:11). Here at last was the long-awaited moment: their encounter with Jesus.

During his time in the seminary, a particularly important process of maturation takes place in the consciousness of the young seminarian: he no longer sees the Church "from the outside," but rather, as it were, "from the inside," and he comes to sense that she is his "home," inasmuch as she is the home of Christ, where "Mary his mother" dwells.

It is Mary who shows him Jesus her Son; she introduces him and in a sense enables him to see and touch Jesus, and to take him into his arms. Mary teaches the seminarian to contemplate Jesus with the eyes of the heart and to make Jesus his very life.

Each moment of seminary life can be an opportunity for loving experience of the presence of Our Lady, who introduces everyone to an encounter with Christ in the silence of meditation, prayer, and fraternity. Mary helps us to meet the Lord above all in the celebration of the Eucharist, when, in the Word and in the consecrated Bread, he becomes our daily spiritual nourishment.

— *Address, Meeting with Seminarians, Cologne, August 19, 2005*

TO THINK ABOUT: Do I remember to ask for Mary's help when I go to meet the Lord in the Eucharist?

GUARD THE MEMORY OF CHRIST

*T*he seminary years are a time of preparing for mission. The Magi "departed for their own country" and most certainly bore witness to their encounter with the King of the Jews.

You too, after your long, necessary program of seminary formation, will be sent forth as ministers of Christ; indeed, each of you will return as an *alter Christus*.

On their homeward journey, the Magi surely had to deal with dangers, weariness, disorientation, doubts. The star was no longer there to guide them! The light was now within them. Their task was to guard and nourish it in the constant memory of Christ, of his Holy Face, of his ineffable Love.

Dear seminarians! One day, God willing, by the consecration of the Holy Spirit you too will begin your mission. Remember always the words of Jesus: "Abide in my love" (Jn 15:9). If you abide close to Christ, with Christ, and in Christ, you will bear much fruit, just as he promised. You have not chosen him — we have just heard this in the witnesses given — he has chosen you (cf. Jn 15:16).

Here is the secret of your vocation and your mission! It is kept in the Immaculate Heart of Mary, who watches over each one of you with a mother's love. Have recourse to Mary, often and with confidence.

— Address, Meeting with Seminarians, Cologne, August 19, 2005

TO THINK ABOUT: What would help me abide in Christ's love more completely? Have I looked to Mary for help?

LEARN LOVE FROM CHRIST

*W*ith special affection I greet you, dear seminarians, and I urge you to respond generously to the call of the Lord and the expectations of the People of God, growing in identification with Christ the High Priest, preparing yourselves for the mission with a solid human, spiritual, theological, and cultural formation. The Seminary is particularly valuable for your future, because, by a full experience and patient work, it leads you to being pastors of souls and teachers of faith, ministers of the holy mysteries and messengers of Christ's charity. Live this time of grace with dedication and cherish in your hearts the joy and dynamism of the first moment of the call and of your "yes," when, responding to Christ's mysterious voice, you gave a decisive turning point to your lives. Be docile to the orders of your superiors and of those responsible for your growth in Christ, and learn from him love for every child of God and of the Church.

— Address, Meeting with Bishops, Priests, Men and Women Religious, and Seminarians, Palermo, October 3, 2010

To think about: What in my seminary formation will stay with me longest? Am I making good use of everything my formation has given me?

DO NOT BE AFRAID

*N*ow, dear brothers and sisters, who can raise the cup of salvation and call on the name of the Lord in the name of the entire people of God, except the priest, ordained for this purpose by his Bishop? At this point, dear inhabitants of Paris and the outlying regions, but also those of you who have come from the rest of France and from neighboring countries, allow me to issue an appeal, confident in the faith and generosity of the young people who are considering a religious or priestly vocation: do not be afraid! Do not be afraid to give your life to Christ! Nothing will ever replace the ministry of priests at the heart of the Church! Nothing will ever replace a Mass for the salvation of the world! Dear young and not so young who are listening to me, do not leave Christ's call unanswered.

— Homily, Notre-Dame, Esplanade des Invalides,
Paris, September 13, 2008

To think about: Have there been times when fear threatened to keep me from my vocation? What helps me overcome that fear?

TWO

A BRIDGE TO GOD

The heart of the Christian faith is the Eucharist, where God himself is present to us in the most intimate way. This is the heart of the priest's ministry — it's actually the heart of what a priest is. The priest is the bridge between God and God's people. Through his ministry, the people of God come face to face with their Lord.

Because of this, people expect to see more than a man when they see a priest. They expect to see an example of true devotion to the Eucharist. The Eucharist is where we meet Christ face to face. When people encounter a priest, they should have that same experience of meeting Christ in person. As the Holy Father says, priests need to become the Eucharist.

Is every priest perfect? Does every priest deserve this honor? No. In reality, no priest deserves it. But this is what the Holy Father calls the "audacity of God": God is far more aware than we are of human weakness, yet he allows weak and fallible human beings to stand for him and act in his name. This is the real glory of the priesthood — a power made perfect in weakness.

THE PRIEST IS A BRIDGE BETWEEN GOD AND MAN

No man on his own, relying on his own power, can put another in touch with God. An essential part of the priest's grace is the gift, the task of creating this contact. This is achieved in the proclamation of God's word in which his light comes to meet us. It is achieved in a particularly concentrated manner in the Sacraments. Immersion in the Paschal Mystery of the death and Resurrection of Christ takes place in Baptism, is reinforced in Confirmation and Reconciliation, and is nourished by the Eucharist, a sacrament that builds the Church as the People of God, Body of Christ, Temple of the Holy Spirit (cf. John Paul II, Apostolic Exhortation *Pastores Gregis*, n. 32). Thus it is Christ himself who makes us holy, that is, who draws us into God's sphere. However, as an act of his infinite mercy, he calls some "to be" with him (cf. Mk 3:14) and to become, through the Sacrament of Orders, despite their human poverty, sharers in his own priesthood, ministers of this sanctification, stewards of his mysteries, "bridges" to the encounter with him and of his mediation between God and man and between man and God (cf. *Presbyterorum Ordinis*, n. 5).

— *General Audience, May 5, 2010*

TO THINK ABOUT: When people come to me, do I lead them toward God? Or do my own human failings sometimes push them away instead?

THE PRIESTHOOD IS NOT SIMPLY "OFFICE," BUT SACRAMENT

*T*he priest is not a mere office-holder, like those that every society needs in order to carry out certain functions. Instead, he does something that no human being can do of his own power: in Christ's name he speaks the words that absolve us of our sins, and in this way he changes, starting with God, our entire life. Over the offerings of bread and wine he speaks Christ's words of thanksgiving, which are words of transubstantiation — words that make Christ himself present, the Risen One, his Body and Blood — words that thus transform the elements of the world, which open the world to God and unite it to him. The priesthood, then, is not simply "office," but sacrament: God makes use of us poor men in order to be, through us, present to all men and women, and to act on their behalf. This audacity of God who entrusts himself to human beings — who, conscious of our weaknesses, nonetheless considers men capable of acting and being present in his stead — this audacity of God is the true grandeur concealed in the word "priesthood."

— Homily at the Conclusion of the Year for Priests,
June 11, 2010

To think about: Do I allow the worldly affairs of my ministry to distract me from my sacramental vocation? How can I reach the right balance between the sacramental priesthood and my very necessary administrative duties?

You can't have proclamation without sacrament

*I*n recent decades there have been tendencies that aim to give precedence, in the priest's identity and mission, to the dimension of proclamation, detaching it from that of sanctification; it is often said that it would be necessary to go beyond a merely sacramental pastoral ministry. Yet, is it possible to exercise the priestly ministry authentically by "going beyond" the sacramental ministry? What exactly does it mean for priests to evangelize, in what does the professed "primacy of proclamation" consist? As the Gospels report, Jesus says that the proclamation of the Kingdom of God is the goal of his mission; this proclamation, however, is not only a "discourse" but at the same time includes his action; the signs and miracles that Jesus works show that the Kingdom comes as a present reality and in the end coincides with his very Person, with his gift of himself. And the same applies for the ordained ministry: he, the priest, represents Christ; he continues his mission, through the "word" and the "sacrament." St. Augustine says: "Let those, therefore, who are servants of Christ, his ministers in word and sacrament, do what he has commanded or permitted" (Letter 228, 2). It is necessary to reflect on whether, in some cases, having underestimated the faithful exercise of the *munus sanctificandi* might not have represented a weakening of faith itself in the salvific efficacy of the sacraments, and, ultimately, in the actual action of Christ and of his Spirit, through the Church, in the world.

— *General Audience, May 5, 2010*

To think about: Am I proclaiming the Kingdom not only in word but in deed as well?

To become the Eucharist

I address you in particular, dear priests, whom Christ has chosen so that with him you may be able to live your life as a sacrifice of praise for the salvation of the world. Only from union with Jesus can you draw that spiritual fruitfulness that generates hope in your pastoral ministry. St. Leo the Great recalls that "our participation in the Body and Blood of Christ aspires to nothing other than to become what we receive" (*Sermo* 12, *De Passione* 3, 7, *PL* 54). If this is true for every Christian it is especially true for us priests. To become the Eucharist! May precisely this be our constant desire and commitment, so that the offering of the Body and Blood of the Lord that we make on the altar may be accompanied by the sacrifice of our existence. Every day, we draw from the Body and Blood of the Lord that free, pure love that makes us worthy ministers of Christ and witnesses to his joy. This is what the faithful expect of the priest: that is, the example of an authentic devotion to the Eucharist; they like to see him spend long periods of silence and adoration before Jesus as was the practice of the Holy Curé d'Ars, whom we shall remember in a special way during the upcoming Year for Priests.

— *Homily, Square Outside the Basilica of St. John Lateran,*
May 11, 2009

To think about: Where am I selfishly holding back from a complete sacrifice of my own existence? What little steps could I take right now to conform myself more completely to the offering of Christ?

INTENSELY EUCHARISTIC SPIRITUALITY

*T*he eucharistic form of the Christian life is seen in a very special way in the priesthood. Priestly spirituality is intrinsically eucharistic. The seeds of this spirituality are already found in the words spoken by the Bishop during the ordination liturgy: "Receive the oblation of the holy people to be offered to God. Understand what you do, imitate what you celebrate, and conform your life to the mystery of the Lord's Cross." In order to give an ever greater eucharistic form to his existence, the priest, beginning with his years in the seminary, should make his spiritual life his highest priority. He is called to seek God tirelessly, while remaining attuned to the concerns of his brothers and sisters. An intense spiritual life will enable him to enter more deeply into communion with the Lord and to let himself be possessed by God's love, bearing witness to that love at all times, even the darkest and most difficult. To this end I join the Synod Fathers in recommending "the daily celebration of Mass, even when the faithful are not present." This recommendation is consistent with the objectively infinite value of every celebration of the Eucharist, and is motivated by the Mass's unique spiritual fruitfulness. If celebrated in a faith-filled and attentive way, Mass is formative in the deepest sense of the word, since it fosters the priest's configuration to Christ and strengthens him in his vocation.

— *Post-Synodical Apostolic Exhortation* Sacramentum Caritatis, *80,*
February 22, 2007

TO THINK ABOUT: When I celebrate Mass, or when I'm present at any Mass, do I always make an effort to understand what I'm doing? Or does the Mass become something to get through?

LIVE THE EUCHARIST INTENSELY

*T*his most holy mystery thus needs to be firmly believed, devoutly celebrated, and intensely lived in the Church. Jesus' gift of himself in the sacrament that is the memorial of his passion tells us that the success of our lives is found in our participation in the trinitarian life offered to us truly and definitively in him. The celebration and worship of the Eucharist enable us to draw near to God's love and to persevere in that love until we are united with the Lord whom we love. The offering of our lives, our fellowship with the whole community of believers, and our solidarity with all men and women are essential aspects of that *logiké latreía*, spiritual worship, holy and pleasing to God (cf. *Rom* 12:1), which transforms every aspect of our human existence, to the glory of God. I therefore ask all pastors to spare no effort in promoting an authentically eucharistic Christian spirituality. Priests, deacons, and all those who carry out a eucharistic ministry should always be able to find in this service, exercised with care and constant preparation, the strength and inspiration needed for their personal and communal path of sanctification. I exhort the lay faithful, and families in particular, to find ever anew in the sacrament of Christ's love the energy needed to make their lives an authentic sign of the presence of the risen Lord. I ask all consecrated men and women to show by their eucharistic lives the splendor and the beauty of belonging totally to the Lord.

— *Post-Synodical Apostolic Exhortation* Sacramentum Caritatis, *94,*
February 22, 2007

TO THINK ABOUT: What do the people around me see in me when they look at my life? Do they see "the splendor and beauty of belonging totally to the Lord"? Or do they see more of my own personal likes and dislikes?

THE CENTER OF MY LIFE

*D*ear priests, the Lord makes us his friends. Therefore, we must be true friends to him. We must want what he wants and not what he does not want. Jesus himself tells us: "You are my friends if you do what I command you" (Jn 15:14). Let this be our common resolution: all of us together, to do his holy will, in which lies our freedom and our joy.

Since the priesthood is rooted in Christ, it is by its nature in the Church and for the Church. Indeed, the Christian faith is not something purely spiritual and internal, nor is our relationship with Christ itself exclusively subjective and private.

Rather, it is a completely concrete and ecclesial relationship. At times, the ministerial priesthood has a constitutive relationship with the Body of Christ in his dual and inseparable dimensions as Eucharist and as Church, as Eucharistic body and Ecclesial body.

In the Eucharistic mystery, Christ gives himself ever anew, and it is precisely in the Eucharist that we learn love of Christ, hence, love for the Church.

I therefore repeat with you, dear brothers in the priesthood, the unforgettable words of John Paul II: "Holy Mass is the absolute center of my life and of every day of my life." And each one of us should be able to say these words are his own: Holy Mass is the absolute center of my life and of my every day.

— *Address to the Clergy of Rome, Basilica of St. John Lateran,*
May 13, 2005

To THINK ABOUT: How does the Mass form the center of my life every day? Or does it? Do other things, worthy and important in themselves, tend to crowd out the Mass?

THE LITURGY DOES NOT BELONG TO US

*T*he "Mystery of Faith": this we proclaim at every Mass. I would like everyone to make a commitment to study this great mystery, especially by revisiting and exploring, individually and in groups, the Council's text on the Liturgy, *Sacrosanctum Concilium*, so as to bear witness courageously to the mystery. In this way, each person will arrive at a better grasp of the meaning of every aspect of the Eucharist, understanding its depth and living it with greater intensity. Every sentence, every gesture has its own meaning and conceals a mystery. I sincerely hope that this Congress will serve as an appeal to all the faithful to make a similar commitment to a renewal of Eucharistic catechesis, so that they themselves will gain a genuine Eucharistic awareness and will in turn teach children and young people to recognize the central mystery of faith and build their lives around it. I urge priests especially to give due honor to the Eucharistic rite, and I ask all the faithful to respect the role of each individual, both priest and lay, in the Eucharistic action. The liturgy does not belong to us: it is the Church's treasure.

— *Homily for the Closing of the 49th International Eucharistic Conference, Québec, June 22, 2008*

To **THINK ABOUT:** Am I always aware of the meaning of every word and gesture in the liturgy? Do I treat the liturgy as a treasure entrusted to me for safekeeping?

THE WORD AND THE BREAD ARE INSEPARABLE

*T*he Holy Spirit, who has led the chosen people by inspiring the authors of the Sacred Scriptures, opens the hearts of believers to understand their meaning. This same Spirit is actively present in the Eucharistic celebration when the priest, "*in persona Christi,*" says the words of consecration, changing the bread and wine into the Body and Blood of Christ, for the spiritual nourishment of the faithful. In order to progress on our earthly pilgrimage towards the heavenly Kingdom, we all need to be nourished by the word and the bread of eternal Life, and these are inseparable from one another!

— Message to the Youth of the World on the Occasion of the 21st World Youth Day, April 9, 2006

TO THINK ABOUT: In my own life and work, are the word and the bread of Life really inseparable? Or do I sometimes neglect one in favor of the other?

No contradiction between editions of the Missal

*T*here is no contradiction between the two editions of the Roman Missal. In the history of the liturgy there is growth and progress, but no rupture. What earlier generations held as sacred, remains sacred and great for us too, and it cannot be all of a sudden entirely forbidden or even considered harmful. It behooves all of us to preserve the riches that have developed in the Church's faith and prayer, and to give them their proper place. Needless to say, in order to experience full communion, the priests of the communities adhering to the former usage cannot, as a matter of principle, exclude celebrating according to the new books. The total exclusion of the new rite would not in fact be consistent with the recognition of its value and holiness.

— Letter to the Bishops on the Occasion of the Publication of the Apostolic Letter "Motu Proprio Data" Summorum Pontificum on the Use of the Roman Liturgy Prior to the Reform of 1970, July 7, 2007

TO THINK ABOUT: The form of the liturgy often brings up intense feelings in Catholics. But do I always put charity and obedience first, even when my own feelings are against the practice of the diocese or the parish?

THE CENTER OF THE CHURCH IS THE EUCHARIST

*I*t is also true that Francis had no intention of creating a new Order, but solely that of renewing the People of God for the Lord who comes. He understood, however, through suffering and pain, that everything must have its own order and that the law of the Church is necessary to give shape to renewal. Thus he placed himself fully, with his heart, in communion with the Church, with the Pope, and with the Bishops. He always knew that the center of the Church is the Eucharist, where the Body of Christ and his Blood are made present through the priesthood, the Eucharist, and the communion of the Church. Wherever the priesthood and the Eucharist and the Church come together, it is there alone that the word of God also dwells. The real historical Francis was the Francis of the Church, and precisely in this way he continues to speak to non-believers and believers of other confessions and religions as well.

— General Audience, Paul VI Audience Hall, January 27, 2010

TO THINK ABOUT: Even when I see something wrong in the Church — and there will always be things wrong in the Church, until the end of time — do I work to correct it with my heart in communion with the Church, the Pope, and the bishops, the way St. Francis did?

*T*o be with Christ — how does this come about? Well, the first and most important thing for the priest is his daily Mass, always celebrated with deep interior participation. If we celebrate Mass truly as men of prayer — if in Communion we let ourselves truly be embraced by him and receive him — then we are being with him.

The Liturgy of the Hours is another fundamental way of being with Christ: here we pray as people conscious of our need to speak with God, while lifting up all those others who have neither the time nor the ability to pray in this way. If our Eucharistic celebration and the Liturgy of the Hours are to remain meaningful, we need to devote ourselves constantly anew to the spiritual reading of sacred Scripture; not only to be able to decipher and explain words from the distant past, but to discover the word of comfort that the Lord is now speaking to me, the Lord who challenges me by this word. Only in this way will we be capable of bringing the inspired Word to the men and women of our time as the contemporary and living Word of God.

Eucharistic adoration is an essential way of being with the Lord. In one of his parables the Lord speaks of a treasure hidden in the field. The hidden treasure is Jesus himself, the Kingdom in person.

— *Homily, Marian Vespers with the Religious and Seminarians of Bavaria, Basilica of Saint Anne, Altötting, September 11, 2006*

TO THINK ABOUT: Do I take advantage of time for Eucharistic adoration?

Devote yourself to the Eucharist

*D*ear seminarians, who have taken the first step towards the priesthood and are preparing in the major seminary or in houses of formation, the Pope encourages you to be conscious of the great responsibility that you will have to assume. Carefully examine your intentions and your motivations. Devote yourselves with a steadfast heart and a generous spirit to your training. The Eucharist, which is the center of Christian life and the school of humility and service, should be your first love. Adoration, piety, and care for the Most Holy Sacrament during these years of preparation will lead you one day to celebrate the Sacrifice of the Altar in an edifying and devout manner.

— *Address, Celebration of Vespers with Priests, Religious, Seminarians, and Deacons, Church of the Most Holy Trinity, Fátima, May 12, 2010*

TO THINK ABOUT: How could I be more devoted to the Eucharist than I already am? What little worldly things stand in my way?

THREE

THE PRIORITY OF PRAYER

Prayer is not an option. It's a necessity.

Without a devotion to constant prayer, a priest simply can't be what God means him to be. It's not enough to show up and do what the book says. You have to know Christ, to be connected to God intimately. And that can only be done with prayer.

So, prayer is at the center of a priest's existence.

I ask you, what are the priorities we should aim for in our ministry as priests and parish priests to avoid fragmentation on the one hand, and on the other, dispersion? Thank you.

The Holy Father: That is a very realistic question, is it not? I am also somewhat familiar with this problem, with all the daily procedures, with all the necessary audiences, with all that there is to do. Yet, it is necessary to determine the right priorities and not to forget the essential: the proclamation of the Kingdom of God. On hearing your question, I remembered the Gospel of two weeks ago on the mission of the 70 disciples. For this first important mission that Jesus had them undertake, the Lord gave them three orders that on the whole I think express the great priorities in the work of a disciple of Christ, a priest, in our day too. The three imperatives are: to pray, to provide care, to preach. I think we should find the balance between these three basic imperatives and keep them ever present as the heart of our work.

— *Meeting with the Clergy of the Dioceses of Belluno-Feltre and Treviso, July 24, 2007*

To THINK ABOUT: How do I balance my priorities? Do the truly important things end up at the top of the list?

JESUS CHRIST COMES FIRST

*T*he Church teaches that priestly ordination is the indispensable condition for the valid celebration of the Eucharist. Indeed, "in the ecclesial service of the ordained minister, it is Christ himself who is present to his Church as Head of his Body, Shepherd of his flock, High Priest of the redemptive sacrifice." Certainly the ordained minister also acts "in the name of the whole Church, when presenting to God the prayer of the Church, and above all when offering the eucharistic sacrifice." As a result, priests should be conscious of the fact that in their ministry they must never put themselves or their personal opinions in first place, but Jesus Christ. Any attempt to make themselves the center of the liturgical action contradicts their very identity as priests. The priest is above all a servant of others, and he must continually work at being a sign pointing to Christ, a docile instrument in the Lord's hands. This is seen particularly in his humility in leading the liturgical assembly, in obedience to the rite, uniting himself to it in mind and heart, and avoiding anything that might give the impression of an inordinate emphasis on his own personality. I encourage the clergy always to see their eucharistic ministry as a humble service offered to Christ and his Church. The priesthood, as Saint Augustine said, is *amoris officium*, it is the office of the good shepherd, who offers his life for his sheep (cf. *Jn* 10:14-15).

— *Post-Synodical Apostolic Exhortation* Sacramentum Caritatis, *23,*
February 22, 2007

TO THINK ABOUT: Where are my own opinions and personality most likely to intrude on my ministry? What do I do to try to keep pointing to Christ instead of to myself?

PRAYER IS YOUR PRIORITY

I know well how difficult it is today — when a priest finds himself directing several parishes and pastoral units; when he must be available to give this or that advice, and so forth — how difficult it is to live such a life. I believe that in this situation it is important to have the courage to limit oneself and to be clear about deciding on priorities. A fundamental priority of priestly life is to be with the Lord, and thus to have time for prayer. St. Charles Borromeo always used to say: "You will not be able to care for the souls of others if you let your own perish. s. You must always have time for being with God." I would therefore like to emphasize: whatever the demands that arise, it is a real priority to find every day an hour to be in silence with the Lord, as the Church suggests we do with the breviary, with daily prayers, so as to return within the reach of the Holy Spirit's breath. And to order priorities on this basis: I must learn to see what is truly essential, where my presence as a priest is indispensable, and where I cannot delegate anyone else. And at the same time, I must humbly accept when there are many things I should do and where my presence is requested that I cannot manage because I know my limits. I think people understand this humility.

*— Meeting with the Clergy of the Diocese of
Bolzano-Bressanone, Cathedral of Bressanone,
August 6, 2008*

To think about: Does my prayer life keep me within the reach of the Holy Spirit's breath? How can I find more time for prayer without neglecting the people who really need my help?

A PROFOUND PERSONAL FRIENDSHIP WITH JESUS

*P*riests must receive preferential attention and paternal care from their Bishops, because they are the primary instigators of authentic renewal of Christian life among the People of God. I should like to offer them a word of paternal affection, hoping that "the Lord will be their portion and cup" (cf. *Ps* 16:5). If the priest has God as the foundation and center of his life, he will experience the joy and the fruitfulness of his vocation. The priest must be above all a "man of God" (*1 Tim* 6:11) who knows God directly, who has a profound personal friendship with Jesus, who shares with others the same sentiments that Christ has (cf. *Phil* 2:5). Only in this way will the priest be capable of leading men to God, incarnate in Jesus Christ, and of being the representative of his love. In order to accomplish his lofty task, the priest must have a solid spiritual formation, and the whole of his life must be imbued with faith, hope, and charity. Like Jesus, he must be one who seeks, through prayer, the face and the will of God, and he must be attentive to his cultural and intellectual preparation.

Dear priests, the Pope accompanies you in your pastoral work and wants you to be full of joy and hope; above all he prays for you.

— Address, Inaugural Session of the Fifth General Conference of the Bishops of Latin America and the Caribbean, May 13, 2007

TO THINK ABOUT: How close have I come to that ideal of a profound personal friendship with the Lord? Is there some way I could devote more time to seeking the face and will of God in prayer?

PRAYER LIFE IS A PRIORITY, NOT AN EXTRA

*T*o be able to to grow, as persons and as priests, it is fundamental first of all to have intimate communion with Christ, whose food was to do the will of his Father (cf. Jn 4:34): all we do is done in communion with him, and we thus rediscover ever anew the unity of our lives in the many facets of our daily occupations.

Let us also learn from the Lord Jesus Christ, who sacrificed himself to do the will of the Father, the art of priestly asceticism that is also necessary today: it should not be exercised on a par with pastoral activities as an additional burden that makes our day even more difficult. On the contrary, we must learn how to surpass ourselves, how to give, and how to offer our lives.

But, if all this is truly to happen within us so that our very action may truly become our self-giving, we need moments in which to replenish our energies, including the physical, and especially to pray and meditate, returning to our inner selves and finding the Lord within us.

Thus, spending time in God's presence in prayer is a real pastoral priority; it is not an addition to pastoral work: being before the Lord is a pastoral priority and, in the final analysis, the most important. John Paul II showed this to us in the most practical and enlightened way in every circumstance of his life and ministry.

— *Address to the Clergy of Rome, Basilica of St. John Lateran,*
May 13, 2005

TO THINK ABOUT: Does prayer seem like a burden to me on top of all the other things I have to do? What could I do to make it seem less of a burden and more of a joy?

LISTEN TO JESUS

I think it is important to be attentive to the Lord's gestures on our journey. He speaks to us through events, through people, through encounters: it is necessary to be attentive to all of this.

Then, a second point, it is necessary to enter into real friendship with Jesus, in a personal relationship with him, and not to know who Jesus is only from others or from books, but to live an ever deeper personal relationship with Jesus, where we can begin to understand what he is asking of us.

And then, the awareness of what I am, of my possibilities: on the one hand, courage, and on the other, humility, trust, and openness, with the help also of friends, of Church authority, and also of priests, of families — what does the Lord want of me?

Of course, this is always a great adventure, but life can be successful only if we have the courage to be adventurous, trusting that the Lord will never leave me alone, that the Lord will go with me and help me.

— Encounter with the Youth of the Diocese of Rome,
St. Peter's Square, April 6, 2006

TO THINK ABOUT: Do I listen to the Lord, not only in the words of Scripture, but also in the voices of the people around me and in the things I see happening every day? What is he trying to tell me in those voices and those events?

BE A MODEL OF PRAYER

*D*ear brother priests, if your faith is to be strong and vigorous, as you well know it must be nourished with assiduous prayer. Thus be models of prayer, become masters of prayer. May your days be marked by times of prayer, during which, after Jesus' example, you engage in a regenerating conversation with the Father. I know it is not easy to stay faithful to this daily appointment with the Lord, especially today when the pace of life is frenetic and worries absorb us more and more. Yet we must convince ourselves: the time he spends in prayer is the most important time in a priest's life, in which divine grace acts with greater effectiveness, making his ministry fruitful. The first service to render to the community is prayer. And therefore, time for prayer must be given a true priority in our life. I know that there are many urgent things: as regards myself, an audience, a document to study, a meeting or something else. But if we are not interiorly in communion with God we cannot even give anything to others. Therefore, God is the first priority. We must always reserve the time necessary to be in communion of prayer with our Lord.

> — *Address to Priests, Deacons, and Seminarians of the Archdiocese of Brindisi, June 15, 2008*

To think about: Do I have particular times set aside for prayer? How often do I allow pressing business to intrude on those times?

RECOGNIZE YOUR WEAKNESS

*I*t is good to recognize one's weakness because in this way we know that we stand in need of the Lord's grace. The Lord comforts us. In the Apostolic College there was not only Judas, but also the good Apostles; yet, Peter fell and many times the Lord reprimanded the Apostles for their slowness, the closure of their hearts, and their scant faith. He therefore simply shows us that none of us is equal to this great yes, equal to celebrating *"in persona Christi,"* to living coherently in this context, to being united to Christ in his priestly mission.

To console us, the Lord has also given us these parables of the net with the good fish and the bad fish, of the field where wheat but also tares grow. He makes us realize that he came precisely to help us in our weakness, and that he did not come, as he says, to call the just, those who claim they are righteous through and through and are not in need of grace, those who pray praising themselves; but he came to call those who know they are lacking, to provoke those who know they need the Lord's forgiveness every day, that they need his grace in order to progress.

— Address, Visit to the Community of the Roman Major Seminary on Occasion of the Feast of Our Lady of Trust, February 17, 2007

TO THINK ABOUT: Where am I weakest? What do I most need the Lord's forgiveness for today?

KNOW GOD INTIMATELY

*N*o one can become a priest by himself; God alone can attract me, can authorize me, can introduce me into participation in Christ's mystery; God alone can enter my life and take me by the hand. This aspect of divine giving, of divine precedence, of divine action that we ourselves cannot bring about and our passivity being chosen and taken by the hand by God is a fundamental point we must enter into. We must always return to the Sacrament, to this gift in which God gives me what I will never be able to give; participation, communion with divine being, with the priesthood of Christ.

Let us also make this reality a practical factor in our life: if this is how it is, a priest must really be a man of God, he must know God intimately and know him in communion with Christ, and so we must live this communion; and the celebration of Holy Mass, the prayer of the Breviary, all our personal prayers are elements of being with God, of being men of God. Our being, our life, and our heart must be fixed in God, in this point from which we must not stir. This is achieved and reinforced day after day with short prayers in which we reconnect with God and become, increasingly, men of God who live in his communion and can thus speak of God and lead people to God.

— *Meeting with the Parish Priests of the Diocese of Rome,*
Hall of Blessings, February 18, 2010

To think about: Are there times in my life when I need to be more passive — more willing to let God go first, to take me by the hand and lead me?

THE CENTRALITY OF CHRIST

*A*s Church and as priests, we proclaim Jesus of Nazareth Lord and Christ, Crucified and Risen, Sovereign of time and of history, in the glad certainty that this truth coincides with the deepest expectations of the human heart. In the mystery of the Incarnation of the Word, that is, of the fact that God became man like us, lies both the content and the method of Christian proclamation. The true dynamic center of the mission is here: in Jesus Christ, precisely. The centrality of Christ brings with it the correct appreciation of the ministerial priesthood, without which there would be neither the Eucharist, nor even the mission nor the Church herself. In this regard it is necessary to be alert to ensure that the "new structures" or pastoral organizations are not planned on the basis of an erroneous interpretation of the proper promotion of the laity for a time in which one would have "to do without" the ordained ministry, because in that case the presuppositions for a further dilution of the ministerial priesthood would be laid and possible presumed "solutions" might come dramatically to coincide with the real causes of contemporary problems linked to the ministry.

— *Address to Members of the Congregation for the Clergy,*
Consistory Hall, March 16, 2009

To think about: When people wonder why we need priests, how do I explain it to them? Or can they see the answer in my own life?

PAY ATTENTION TO GOD'S SIGNS

*A*s Jesus did with the deaf-mute, God continues likewise to reveal to us his project through "events and words." Listening to his word and discerning his signs must therefore be the task of every Christian and every community. The most immediate of God's signs is undoubtedly attention to one's neighbor in accordance with what Jesus said: "As you did it to one of the least of these my brethren, you did it to me" (Mt 25:40). Furthermore, as the Second Vatican Council affirmed, the Christian is called to be "a witness before the world to the resurrection and life of the Lord Jesus, and a sign of the living God" (*Lumen Gentium*, n. 38). The priest whom Christ has chosen all for himself must be such in the first place. During this Year for Priests, pray with greater intensity for priests, for seminarians, and for vocations, so that they may be faithful to this vocation of theirs! Likewise, every consecrated and every baptized person must be a sign of the living God.

— *Homily, Eucharistic Concelebration, Valle Faul,*
Viterbo, September 6, 2009

TO THINK ABOUT: How am I a sign of God's intentions to the people around me? How are they signs to me? If I think and watch carefully, do I notice any signs I've been missing?

FIDELITY IS YOUR GREATEST CONCERN

*L*et me open my heart and tell you that the greatest concern of every Christian, especially of every consecrated person or minister of the altar, must be fidelity, loyalty to one's own vocation, as a disciple who wishes to follow the Lord. Faithfulness over time is the name of love, of a consistent, true, and profound love for Christ the Priest. "Since Baptism is a true entry into the holiness of God through incorporation into Christ and the indwelling of his Spirit, it would be a contradiction to settle for a life of mediocrity, marked by a minimalistic ethic and a shallow religiosity" (John Paul II, Apostolic Letter *Novo Millennio Ineunte*, n. 31). In this Year for Priests, which is drawing to its close, may grace in abundance come down upon you that you may live joyfully your consecration and bear witness to your priestly fidelity grounded in the fidelity of Christ. This evidently supposes true intimacy with Christ in prayer, since it is the powerful and intense experience of the Lord's love that brings priests and consecrated persons to respond to his love in way that is exclusive and spousal.

— *Address, Celebration of Vespers with Priests, Religious, Seminarians, and Deacons, Church of the Most Holy Trinity, Fátima, May 12, 2010*

To think about: What would change in my life if I were *more* loyal to my vocation?

FOUR

LIVING IN THE BODY OF CHRIST

We are all members of the Body of Christ, and no priest lives outside the organization of the Church. Living in that community is part of the priestly mission, but it's not a skill everyone is born with.

It can be hard getting along with other people — even other priests. It can even be hard getting along with bishops. As long as we're living in this fallen world, our own desires and petty jealousies will always be coming into conflict with everyone else's.

But how can we model the life of Christ to the laity if we can't get along ourselves?

The Holy Father's advice on this subject is both spiritual and practical. He knows as well as anyone the difficulties of dealing with the Church hierarchy — he's seen the hierarchy from both ends. But he also knows the vital importance of unity. And he knows the encouraging comfort of realizing that, as a priest, you're not in it alone.

Unity is work. No one knows that better than the Holy Father. But it's also a source of great strength that makes the work worthwhile. The community of the priesthood, instead of being a source of frustration, will become a great joy, as long as the members of that community do the work that goes into keeping themselves a community.

NEVER ALONE

*T*he motto of these days has been: "those who believe are never alone." These words apply and must apply especially to priests, to each one of us. They apply in two senses: a priest is never alone because Jesus Christ is always with him. He is with us, let us also be with him! But they must apply in another sense too. He who becomes a priest enters into a presbyterate, a community of priests together with their Bishop. He is a priest in this communion with his confrères. Let us commit ourselves to live this out, not only as a theological and juridical precept, but also as a practical experience for each of us. Let us offer this communion to one another, let us offer it especially to those that we know are suffering from loneliness, those that we know are troubled by questions and problems, and perhaps by doubts and uncertainties! Let us offer this communion to each other, and so experience our communion with Jesus Christ ever anew, more fully and more joyfully, through being with the other, through being with others! Amen.

— Address, Meeting with Priests and Permanent Deacons of Bavaria, Cathedral of St. Mary and St. Corbinian, September 14, 2006

To think about: Am I troubled by loneliness myself? Can I see some of the same symptoms in some of my brothers? Can I use that knowledge to help both them and myself?

The grace of perseverance

*I*t is also important of course not to isolate oneself, not to believe one is capable of going ahead alone. We truly need the company of priest friends and also lay friends who accompany and help us. It is very important for a priest, in the parish itself, to see how people trust in him and to experience in addition to their trust also their generosity in pardoning his weaknesses. True friends challenge us and help us to be faithful on our journey. It seems to me that this attitude of patience and humility can help us to be kind to others, to understand the weaknesses of others and also help them to forgive as we forgive.

I think I am not being indiscreet if I say that today I received a beautiful letter from Cardinal Martini: I had congratulated him on his 80th birthday — we are the same age; in thanking me he wrote: "I thank the Lord above all for the gift of perseverance. Today," he writes, "good is done rather *ad tempus, ad experimentum.* Good, in accordance with its essence, can only be done definitively; but to do it definitively we need the grace of perseverance. I pray each day," he concluded, "that the Lord will grant me this grace."

— *Address, Visit to the Community of the Roman Major Seminary on Occasion of the Feast of Our Lady of Trust, February 17, 2007*

To think about: Am I at least as willing to pardon the weaknesses of others as they are to pardon mine? Would exercising a little humility and understanding my own weaknesses help me overcome some of my lingering resentments?

KEEP COMMUNICATION OPEN

*T*he different levels of the hierarchy too — from the parish priest to the Bishop, to the Supreme Pontiff — must continually exchange ideas with one another, they must foster dialogue to find together the best road. The experiences of parish priests are fundamental, and so are the experiences of the Bishop, and let us say, the universal perspectives of the Pope have a theological and pastoral place of their own in the Church.

On the one hand, these different levels of the hierarchy as a whole, and on the other, all life as it is lived in the parish context with patience and openness in obedience to the Lord, really create new vitality in the Church.

— Address, Lenten Meeting with the Clergy of Rome,
Hall of Blessings, February 22, 2007

TO THINK ABOUT: Do I keep up my part of the communication? Or does important information fall into me as if I were a black hole, either because of fear or through laziness?

SENT OUT, BUT STILL WITH HIM

*W*here do we go if we say "yes" to the Lord's call? The briefest description of the priestly mission — and this is true in its own way for men and women religious also — has been given to us by the Evangelist Mark. In his account of the call of the Twelve, he says: "Jesus appointed twelve to be with him and to be sent out" (3:14). To be with Jesus and, being sent, to go out to meet people — these two things belong together, and together they are the heart of a vocation, of the priesthood. To be with him and to be sent out — the two are inseparable. Pope Gregory the Great, in one of his homilies, once said that God's angels, however far afield they go on their missions, always move in God. They remain always with him. And while speaking about the angels, Saint Gregory thought also of bishops and priests: wherever they go, they should always "be with him." We know this from experience: whenever priests, because of their many duties, allot less and less time to being with the Lord, they eventually lose, for all their often heroic activity, the inner strength that sustains them. Their activity ends up as an empty activism.

— *Homily, Marian Vespers with the Religious and Seminarians of Bavaria,*
Basilica of Saint Anne, Altötting, September 11, 2006

TO THINK ABOUT: Even when I'm "sent" on my daily mission — when I'm overwhelmingly busy — do I still remain with the Lord in my heart?

There is no place for division

The coming Synod of Bishops for Africa will address among other themes the topic of ethnic unrest. The marvelous image of the Heavenly Jerusalem, the gathering of innumerable men and women from every tribe and tongue and people and nation who have been ransomed by the blood of Christ (cf. *Rev* 5:9), encourages you to confront the challenge of ethnic conflict wherever present, even within the Church. I express my appreciation to those of you who have accepted a pastoral mission outside the limits of your own regional or linguistic group, and I thank the priests and people who have welcomed and supported you. Your readiness to adapt to others is an eloquent sign that as the new family of all who believe in Christ (cf. *Mk* 3:31-35) there is no place in the Church for any kind of division. Catechumens and neophytes must be taught to accept this truth as they make their commitment to Christ and to a life of Christian love. All believers, especially seminarians and priests, will grow in maturity and generosity by allowing the Gospel message to purify and overcome any possible narrowness of local perspectives.

— Address to the Bishops of Nigeria on Their "Ad Limina" Visit,
Consistory Hall, February 14, 2009

To think about: Where do I see division in the Catholic Christians around me? How can I help overcome that division?

JOIN FORCES WITH OTHER PRIESTS

*D*ear brother priests, in this place, which Mary has made special, keep before your eyes her vocation as a faithful disciple of her Son Jesus from the moment of his conception to the Cross, and then beyond, along the path of the nascent Church, and consider the unheard-of grace of your priesthood. Fidelity to one's vocation requires courage and trust, but the Lord also wishes that you join forces: that you be concerned for one another and support one another fraternally. Moments of common prayer and study, and sharing in the demands of the priestly life and work, are a necessary part of your life. It is a fine thing when you welcome one another into your homes with the peace of Christ in your hearts! It is important to assist one another with prayer, helpful advice, and discernment! Be especially attentive to those situations where there is a certain weakening of priestly ideals or dedication to activities not fully consonant with what is proper for a minister of Jesus Christ. Then is the time to take a firm stand, with an attitude of warm fraternal love, as brother assisting his brother, to "remain on his feet."

— Address, Celebration of Vespers with Priests, Religious, Seminarians, and Deacons, Church of the Most Holy Trinity, Fátima, May 12, 2010

To think about: Even when my work seems overwhelming, is there time in my life to encourage others in the same situation and to be encouraged by them? How could I rearrange my priorities to make more time for my brothers?

I must say that when I became Archbishop of Munich I did not find more than perhaps three or four deacons. I have strongly encouraged this ministry because it seems to me that it enhances the riches of the Church's sacramental ministry. At the same time, it can also serve as a link between the secular world, the professional world, and the world of the priestly ministry, since many deacons continue to carry out their professions and keep their posts — both important and also simple positions — while on Saturdays and Sundays they work in church. Thus, they witness in the contemporary world as well as in the world of work to the presence of the faith, the sacramental ministry, and the diaconal dimension of the Sacrament of Orders. I consider this very important: the visibility of the diaconal dimension.

Every priest, of course, also continues to be a deacon and must always be aware of this dimension, for the Lord himself became our minister, our deacon. Recall the act of the washing of the feet, where it is explicitly shown that the Teacher, the Lord, acts as a deacon and wants those who follow him to be deacons and carry out this ministry for humanity, to the point that they even help us to wash the dirty feet of the people entrusted to our care. This dimension seems to me to be of paramount importance.

— *Address, Meeting with the Parish Priests and Clergy of the Diocese of Rome, Hall of Blessings, February 7, 2008*

TO THINK ABOUT: How do I encourage the diaconal ministry in my own parish?

DEALING WITH HEAVIER BURDENS

*T*he number of priests has declined even if at the present moment we are able to cope. To be looking after two, three, or four parishes at the same time, in addition to all the new tasks that have emerged, can lead to discouragement. Often I ask myself how are we going to cope? Is this not a profession that no longer brings us joy since we see that whatever we do is never enough?

It is necessary to combine zeal with humility, with an awareness of our limitations We feel impelled to go out to the poor, the elderly, the weak, to children and young people, to those in their prime. Yet our zeal, lest it become empty and begin to wear us down, must be combined with humility, with moderation, with the acceptance of our limits. So many things should be done, yet I see that I am not capable of doing them. This is true, I imagine, for many pastors, and it is also true for the Pope, who ought to do so many things! My strength is simply not enough. In this way I learn to do what I can, and I leave the rest to God.

— Address, Meeting with Priests and Permanent Deacons of Bavaria, Cathedral of St. Mary and St. Corbinian, September 14, 2006

To think about: When I'm overwhelmed in my work, do I have the humility to ask God for help? And then do I have the humility to trust the work to the helpers God sends me — even if they won't do it exactly the way I would do it?

SERVANTS OF JOY

*D*ear friends, this is also your mission: to bring the Gospel to everyone so that everyone may experience the joy of Christ and that there be joy in every city. What can be more beautiful than this? What can be greater, more exciting, than cooperating in spreading the Word of life in the world, than communicating the living water of the Holy Spirit? To proclaim and to witness joy: this is the central core of your mission, dear deacons who will soon become priests. The Apostle Paul called Gospel ministers "servants of joy." He wrote in his Second Letter to the Christians of Corinth: "Domineering over your faith is not my purpose. I prefer to work with you toward your happiness. As regards faith, you are standing firm" (2 Cor 1:24). These are programmatic words for every priest. In order to be collaborators in the joy of others, in a world that is often sad and negative, the fire of the Gospel must burn within you and the joy of the Lord dwell in you. Only then will you be able to be messengers and multipliers of this joy, bringing it to all, especially to those who are sorrowful and disheartened.

— *Homily, Ordination of New Priests for the Diocese of Rome,*
St. Peter's Basilica, April 27, 2008

TO THINK ABOUT: Do the people around me experience the joy of Christ in my work? Or do they see only the burdens of my duties?

PASS THE CALL ON

*I*n order that the People of God may never lack ministers to give them the Body of Christ, we must ask the Lord to make the gift of new priests to his Church. I also ask you to pass on the call to the priesthood to young men, so that they will joyfully and fearlessly respond to the Lord. They will not be disappointed. May the family be the origin and cradle of vocations.

— Homily for the Closing of the 49th International Eucharistic Conference,
Québec, June 22, 2008

To think about: What am I doing to encourage vocations? Where are opportunities in my own parish?

FIVE

CELIBACY

The world finds it harder to understand celibacy than any other aspect of the priesthood. Yet celibacy is not intended to be what the world sees it as: an endless and painful privation. It's meant to be a sign and a foretaste of the ineffable joys of heaven. In priestly celibacy, the Holy Father says, "the future world of God enters into the reality of our time." In his joyously celibate life, the priest shows the world what heaven is like.

This is the thing the world, obsessed with sex and instant gratification, finds hardest to understand. Yet it is precisely because the world has lost the sense that there is anything beyond momentary pleasure that the celibacy of the priesthood is a valuable prophetic sign. In the midst of the world, as it reels from one disappointment to the next in its endless quest for gratification, are men who live a life devoted to something permanent, something that will never disappoint us.

Celibacy — like any other form of self-denial — is not easy in a world full of temptations. Yet the celibate priest can find strength in knowing that he gives up something good for something infinitely better. He is a sign, here in the fallen world, that points to heaven, and nothing makes the message clearer than his own visible rejection of what the world calls most valuable.

CELIBACY, AN ANTICIPATION OF THE FUTURE LIFE

*O*ne great problem of Christianity in today's world is that it does not think anymore of the future of God. The present of this world alone seems sufficient. We want to have only this world, to live only in this world. So we close the doors to the true greatness of our existence. The meaning of celibacy as an anticipation of the future is to open these doors, to make the world greater, to show the reality of the future that should be lived by us already as present. Living, then, as a testimony of faith: we truly believe that God exists, that God enters into my life, and that I can found my life on Christ, on the future life. It is true that for the agnostic world, the world in which God does not enter, celibacy is a great scandal, because it shows exactly that God is considered and experienced as reality. With the eschatological dimension of celibacy, the future world of God enters into the reality of our time. And should this disappear?

— *Dialogue with Priests, St. Peter's Square, June 10, 2010*

To think about: Do people around me see my life as a testament to the reality of God? Or do they see mostly the burdens under which I struggle? How could I make the joy more visible?

CELIBACY, THE DEFINITIVE "YES"

*I*n a certain sense, this continuous criticism against celibacy may surprise in a time when it is becoming increasingly fashionable not to get married. But this not-getting married is something totally, fundamentally different from celibacy. The avoidance of marriage is based on a will to live only for oneself, and therefore a "no" to the bond, While celibacy is just the opposite: it is a definitive "yes," It is to give oneself into the hands of the Lord. And therefore, it is an act of loyalty and trust, an act that also implies the fidelity of marriage. And this marriage is the foundation of the great Christian culture. And if that disappears, the root of our culture will be destroyed. So, we want to go ahead and make present this scandal of a faith that bases all existence on God. We know that besides this great scandal that the world does not want to recognize, there are also the secondary scandals of our shortcomings, which make people think, "They are not really living on the foundation of God." But there is also so much loyalty! Celibacy is a great sign of faith, of the presence of God in the world. We pray to the Lord to help us, to set us free from the secondary scandals in order to make relevant the great scandal of our faith: the confidence, the strength of our life, which is founded in God and in Jesus Christ!

— *Dialogue with Priests, St. Peter's Square, June 10, 2010*

To think about: Do I hang on to some faults that make people wonder if I am "really living on the foundation of God"?

THE PROPHETIC VALUE OF CELIBACY

*D*uring the last fifty years, the Church in China has never lacked an abundant flowering of vocations to the priesthood and to consecrated life. For this we must thank the Lord, because it is a sign of vitality and a reason for hope.

I am aware, however, that this flowering is accompanied, today, by not a few difficulties. The need therefore emerges both for more careful vocational discernment on the part of Church leaders, and for more in-depth education and instruction of aspirants to the priesthood and religious life. Notwithstanding the precariousness of the means available, for the future of the Church in China it will be necessary to take steps to ensure, on the one hand, particular attention in the care of vocations and, on the other hand, a more solid formation with regard to the human, spiritual, philosophical-theological, and pastoral aspects, to be carried out in seminaries and religious institutes. In this regard, the formation for celibacy of candidates for the priesthood deserves particular mention. It is important that they learn to live and to esteem celibacy as a precious gift from God and as an eminently eschatological sign that bears witness to an undivided love for God and for his people, and configures the priest to Jesus Christ, Head and Bridegroom of the Church. This gift, in fact, in an outstanding way "expresses the priest's service to the Church in and with the Lord" and has a prophetic value for today's world.

— Letter to the Bishops, Priests, Consecrated Persons, and Lay Faithful of the Catholic Church in the People's Republic of China, May 27, 2007

TO THINK ABOUT: How do I view celibacy? Do I see it as a divine gift and a sign of undivided love for God?

SIX

Leading
by
Example

The priest doesn't just preach virtue: he models the Christian life for everyone he meets, whether in his parish or anywhere else in the world. A priest is a walking billboard that says, "This is how a Christian lives."

For that reason, the Holy Father says, a priest always needs to keep in mind that people's eyes are on him. They expect him to be an expert in living the Christian life. That's true wherever they meet him, which is why being a priest can never be just a job.

Humility is a very important part of the example a priest sets. You may have had grand ideas about the good you were going to accomplish, and it may seem to you that you're stuck in an inconsequential place with no room for greatness. But that may be precisely your greatness: that, sharing Christ's humility, you show the world a man who lives for Christ, not for himself.

Above all, the priest needs to show the world that living for Christ is a joy. The world has many joys to offer — fleeting joys, and often ones that carry a heavy price, but joys that are clearly visible. It's up to priests to make the joy of Christian life even more plainly visible to a world that's forgotten how to live for anything but the present.

HUMILITY COMES FIRST

I would say, then, that firstly, what is necessary for all of us is to recognize our own limitations, to humbly recognize that we have to leave most things to the Lord. Today, we heard in the Gospel the Parable of the Faithful Servant (Mt 24:42-51). This servant, the Lord tells us, gives food to the others at the proper time. He does not do everything at once but is a wise and prudent servant who knows what needs to be done in a specific situation. He does so humbly, and is also sure of his master's trust. So it is that we must likewise do our utmost to be wise and prudent and to trust in the goodness of our "Master," the Lord, for in the end it is he himself who must take the helm of his Church. We fit into her with our small gift and do the best we can, especially those things that are always necessary: celebrating the sacraments, preaching the Word, giving signs of our charity and our love.

— Meeting with the Priests of the Diocese of Albano,
August 31, 2006

TO THINK ABOUT: Am I often tempted to take on more than I should be responsible for? How can I keep to the way of humble obedience without neglecting my real responsibilities?

IT'S NOT JUST A JOB

I think that, above all, it is important that the faithful can see that the priest does not just perform a "job" with working hours, and then is free and lives only for himself, but that he is a passionate man of Christ who carries in himself the fire of Christ's love. If the faithful see that he is full of the joy of the Lord and understand also that he cannot do everything, they can accept limits and help the parish priest. This seems to me the most important point: that we can see and feel that the parish priest really feels his call from the Lord, that he is full of love for the Lord and for his faithful. If there is this, you understand and you can also see the impossibility of doing everything. So, being full of the joy of the Gospel with our whole being is the first condition.

— *Dialogue with Priests, St. Peter's Square, June 10, 2010*

TO THINK ABOUT: If people in my parish were asked about how I conduct my priestly service, what would they say? What facts about my life would support their observations?

LIVE A LIFE THAT DRAWS PEOPLE TO PENANCE

*E*very priest becomes a minister of Penance through his ontological configuration to Christ, the Eternal High Priest, who reconciles humanity with the Father; so the priest is charged with the responsibility of faithfully administering the Sacrament of Reconciliation.

We live in a cultural context marked by the hedonistic and relativistic mindset that tends to delete God from the horizon of life and does not encourage the acquisition of a clear set of values to refer to that would help one to discern good from evil and develop a proper sense of sin.

This situation makes even more urgent the service of stewards of Divine Mercy. We must not forget, in fact, that a sort of vicious circle exists between the clouding of the experience of God and the loss of the sense of sin.... In the conditions of freedom in which it is now possible to exercise the priestly ministry, priests must live the response to their vocation "in a lofty manner," for only those who become every day a living and clear presence of the Lord can awaken in the faithful a sense of sin, impart courage, and give rise to the desire for God's forgiveness.

— *To Participants in the Course on the Internal Forum Organized by the Apostolic Penitentiary, March 11, 2010*

To think about: What do the people around me see when they look at my way of living? Does my example give them the courage to repent and confess their sins?

EXPERT IN THE SPIRITUAL LIFE

*T*he faithful expect only one thing from priests: that they be specialists in promoting the encounter between man and God. The priest is not asked to be an expert in economics, construction or politics. He is expected to be an expert in the spiritual life. With this end in view, when a young priest takes his first steps, he needs to be able to refer to an experienced teacher who will help him not to lose his way among the many ideas put forward by the culture of the moment. In the face of the temptations of relativism or the permissive society, there is absolutely no need for the priest to know all the latest, changing currents of thought; what the faithful expect from him is that he be a witness to the eternal wisdom contained in the revealed word. Solicitude for the quality of personal prayer and for good theological formation bears fruit in life. Living under the influence of totalitarianism may have given rise to an unconscious tendency to hide under an external mask, and in consequence to become somewhat hypocritical. Clearly this does not promote authentic fraternal relations and may lead to an exaggerated concentration on oneself. In reality, we grow in affective maturity when our hearts adhere to God. Christ needs priests who are mature, virile, capable of cultivating an authentic spiritual paternity. For this to happen, priests need to be honest with themselves, open with their spiritual director, and trusting in divine mercy.

— *Address, Meeting with the Clergy, Warsaw Cathedral, May 25, 2006*

TO THINK ABOUT: How honest am I with my spiritual director? With myself? Do the people around me see that honesty when they compare what I say to what I do?

BEING TRULY REASONABLE

*P*rudence, according to the Greek philosophical tradition, is the first of the cardinal virtues. It indicates the primacy of the truth, which, through "prudence," becomes a criterion for our action. Prudence demands humble, disciplined, and watchful reason that does not let itself be blinded by prejudices; it does not judge according to desires and passions but rather seeks the truth, even though it may prove uncomfortable. Prudence means searching for the truth and acting in conformity with it. The prudent servant is first and foremost a man of truth and a man of sincere reason. God, through Jesus Christ, has opened wide for us the window of the truth, which, before our own mere forces, often remains narrow and only partially transparent. In Sacred Scripture and in faith in the Church God shows us the essential truth about man, which impresses the right orientation upon our action. Thus, the first cardinal virtue of the priest as minister of Jesus Christ consists in letting himself be molded by the truth that Christ shows us. In this way we become truly reasonable people, who judge on the basis of the whole and not on chance details. Let us not allow ourselves to be guided by what we see through the small window of our personal astuteness, but, rather, let us look at the world and at human beings through the large window that Christ has opened to us on the whole truth and thus recognize what truly counts in life.

— *Homily, Mass for the Episcopal Ordination of Five New Bishops,*
Vatican Basilica, September 12, 2009

TO THINK ABOUT: How do I know when my prejudices are blinding me to the truth? Whom do I trust to warn me when my own desires have hijacked my power of reason?

SOW TRUST AND HOPE

*T*here is another saying of Jesus' that uses the image of the seed, and that can accompany the Parable of the Sower: "Unless a grain of wheat falls into the earth and dies, it remains alone; but if it dies, it bears much fruit" (Jn 12:24). Here the Lord insists on the connection between the death of the seed and the "much fruit" that it will yield. The grain of wheat is he, Jesus. The fruit is having "life abundantly" (Jn 10:10), which he acquired for us through his Cross. This is also the logic and the true fruitfulness of every vocations ministry in the Church. Like Christ, the priest and the animator must be a "grain of wheat" who sacrifices itself to do the Father's will; who lives hidden from the clamor and the noise; who renounces the search for that visibility and grandiose image that today often become the criteria and even goals of life in a large part of our culture and that attract many young people.

Dear friends, be sowers of trust and hope. The word of God can truly become light and strength, a spring of hope, it can plot a path that passes through Jesus, the "path" and the "way"; through his Cross, which is the fullness of love.

— Address to Participants in the European Congress
on the Pastoral Care of Vocations,
Clementine Hall, July 4, 2009

TO THINK ABOUT: What sacrifices do I need to make to "die" to my own will, like the grain of wheat? Which of popular culture's goals and distinctions are most tempting to me?

LIVING WITH CHRIST FOR EVERYONE

*I*mmediately after his forced ordination, Augustine wrote to Bishop Valerius: "I was constrained ... to accept second place at the helm, when as yet I knew not how to handle an oar.... And from this derived the tears that some of my brethren perceived me shedding in the city at the time of my ordination" (cf. *Letter* 21, 1ff.).

Augustine's beautiful dream of a contemplative life had vanished. As a result, his life had fundamentally changed. He could now no longer dedicate himself solely to meditation in solitude. He had to live with Christ for everyone. He had to express his sublime knowledge and thoughts in the thoughts and language of the simple people in his city. The great philosophical work of an entire lifetime, of which he had dreamed, was to remain unwritten.

Instead, however, we have been given something far more precious: the Gospel translated into the language of everyday life and of his sufferings.

— *Homily, "Orti Borromaici" Esplanade, Pavia, April 22, 2007*

To THINK ABOUT: How is the actuality of my vocation different from the way I had imagined it? Why might God be pushing me in *this* direction instead of *that* direction?

To attract all to communion

*S*t. Paul thus said in Romans, chapter 15: "The grace given me by God to be 'a minister' of Christ Jesus to the Gentiles in the priestly service (*hierourgein*) of the Gospel of God, so that the offering of the Gentiles may be acceptable, sanctified by the Holy Spirit" (15:15ff.). I would like to emphasize only two aspects of this marvelous text. First of all, St. Paul interprets his missionary activity among the world's peoples to build the universal Church as priestly service. To proclaim the Gospel in order to unite the peoples in the communion of the Risen Christ is a "priestly" action. The apostle of the Gospel is a true priest, he does what is central to the priesthood: prepares the true sacrifice. And then the second aspect: the goal of missionary action is we can say the cosmic liturgy: that the peoples united in Christ, the world, may as such become the glory of God, an "acceptable [offering], sanctified by the Holy Spirit." Here the dynamic aspect appears, the aspect of hope in the Pauline conception of worship: Christ's gift of himself implies the aspiration to attract all to communion in his body, to unite the world. Only in communion with Christ, the exemplary man, one with God, does the world thus become as we all wish it to be: a mirror of divine love. This dynamism is ever present in the Eucharist; this dynamism must inspire and form our life.

— General Audience, Paul VI Audience Hall, January 7, 2009

To think about: What about me and what I do attracts people separated from the Church to communion? Can they see, through me, what I love in the liturgy?

*C*ertainly within the Church's divinely-willed structure there is a distinction to be made between hierarchical and charismatic gifts (cf. *Lumen Gentium*, 4). Yet the very variety and richness of the graces bestowed by the Spirit invite us constantly to discern how these gifts are to be rightly ordered in the service of the Church's mission. You, dear priests, by sacramental ordination have been configured to Christ, the Head of the Body. You, dear deacons, have been ordained for the service of that Body. You, dear men and women religious, both contemplative and apostolic, have devoted your lives to following the divine Master in generous love and complete devotion to his Gospel. All of you, who fill this cathedral today, as well as your retired, elderly, and infirm brothers and sisters, who unite their prayers and sacrifices to your labors, are called to be forces of unity within Christ's Body. By your personal witness, and your fidelity to the ministry or apostolate entrusted to you, you prepare a path for the Spirit. For the Spirit never ceases to pour out his abundant gifts, to awaken new vocations and missions, and to guide the Church, as our Lord promised in this morning's Gospel, into the fullness of truth (cf. *Jn* 16:13).

— *Homily, Votive Mass for the Universal Church,*
St. Patrick's Cathedral, New York, April 19, 2008

To think about: What gifts have been given to me to use in the Lord's service? How are they most useful in the place I've been sent to serve?

You are a foretaste of heaven

*T*his life of special consecration was born to keep the Gospel always before the People of God, as a reminder that manifests, certifies, and proclaims to the whole Church the radical nature of the Gospel and the coming of the Kingdom. Dear consecrated men and women, by your dedication to prayer, asceticism, and growth in the spiritual life, to apostolic action and mission, you are progressing towards the heavenly Jerusalem, you are a foretaste of the eschatological Church, solid in her possession and loving contemplation of God who is love. How much we need this witness today! Many of our brothers and sisters live as if there were nothing beyond this life, and without concern for their eternal salvation. Men and women are called to know and love God, and the Church has the mission to assist them in this calling. We know well that God is the master of his gifts and that conversion is a grace. But we are responsible for proclaiming the faith, the whole faith, with all its demands. Dear friends, let us imitate the Curé of Ars who prayed to the Lord in the following words: "Grant me the conversion of my parish, and I accept to suffer all that you wish for the rest of my life." And he did everything to pull people away from their own lukewarm attitude in order to lead them back to love.

— Address, Celebration of Vespers with Priests, Religious, Seminarians, and Deacons, Church of the Most Holy Trinity, Fátima, May 12, 2010

To think about: Do people see through me to the life beyond this life? Or is that life hidden behind the cares and responsibilities of my daily work?

THE ATTRACTIVE ASPECT OF VIRTUE

*T*here exists a deep solidarity among all the members of the Body of Christ. It is not possible to love Christ without loving his brothers and sisters. For their salvation John Mary Vianney decided to become a priest: "to win souls for the good God," as he said when, at eighteen years of age, he announced his vocation, just as Paul had said: "to win as many as I could" (1 Cor 9:19). The Vicar General had told him: "there is not much love of God in the parish; you will bring it there." In his priestly passion, this holy parish priest was merciful like Jesus in meeting each sinner. He preferred to insist on the attractive aspect of virtue, on God's mercy, in comparison to which our sins are like "grains of sand." He pointed to the merciful love of God, which had been offended. He feared that priests would become "insensitive" and accustomed to the indifference of their faithful: "Woe to the Pastor — he would warn — who remains silent while God is offended and souls are lost."

— Address, Celebration of Vespers with Priests, Religious,
Seminarians, and Deacons, Church of the Most Holy Trinity,
Fátima, May 12, 2010

TO THINK ABOUT: In the name of "mercy," have I become insensitive to the indifference of the people I am responsible for? How can I warn people to avoid serious wrongdoing in a loving way?

You must be truly human

The other element is that the priest must be man, human in all senses. That is, he must live true humanity, true humanism; he must be educated, have a human formation, human virtues; he must develop his intelligence, his will, his sentiments, his affections; he must be a true man, a man according to the will of the Creator, of the Redeemer, for we know that the human being is wounded and the question of "what man is" is obscured by the event of sin that hurt human nature even to the quick. Thus people say: "he lied," "it is human"; "he stole," "it is human" — but this is not really being human. Human means being generous, being good, being a just person, it means true prudence and wisdom. Therefore emerging with Christ's help from this dark area in our nature so as to succeed in being truly human in the image of God is a lifelong process that must begin in our training for the priesthood. It must subsequently be achieved, however, and continue as long as we live.

— *Meeting with the Parish Priests of the Diocese of Rome,*
Hall of Blessings, February 18, 2010

To think about: How well does the prudence and wisdom I preach translate to my daily practice?

SEVEN

SUFFERING

We all have bad times. Suffering is part of the human condition in our fallen world. But how can you lead others to the joy of Christ when you're not feeling joyful yourself?

The Holy Father's daring answer is that the suffering itself is cause for joy. When you suffer, he says, you need to remember that you're sharing a little bit in the greater sufferings of Christ. And deserving to share Christ's suffering is an indescribable privilege. Anyone who suffers with Christ will also share in Christ's glory.

The key is to love with Christ as well as suffer with him. The yoke that seems unbearably heavy gets lighter and lighter as love grows stronger in your heart.

And the way to grow that love is through prayer. Bring the sufferings of the world to God. Don't just accept the cross, but embrace it. By emptying yourself out along with Christ, you enter into the mystery of Christ. And that's what makes you ready to proclaim that mystery to the world.

Rejoice when you suffer

*I*n this Year for Priests, let me address a special word to the priests present today, and to those who are preparing for ordination. Reflect on the words spoken to a newly ordained priest as the Bishop presents him with the chalice and paten: "Understand what you do, imitate what you celebrate, and conform your life to the mystery of the Lord's Cross." As we proclaim the Cross of Christ, let us always strive to imitate the selfless love of the one who offered himself for us on the altar of the Cross, the one who is both priest and victim, the one in whose person we speak and act when we exercise the ministry that we have received. As we reflect on our shortcomings, individually and collectively, let us humbly acknowledge that we have merited the punishment that he, the innocent Lamb, suffered on our behalf. And if, in accordance with what we have deserved, we should have some share in Christ's sufferings, let us rejoice because we will enjoy a much greater gladness when his glory is revealed.

— *Homily, Holy Mass Attended by Priests, Religious, Deacons, Catechists and Representatives of Cyprian Ecclesial Movements, June 5, 2010*

TO THINK ABOUT: It's all very well to *say* that I rejoice when I suffer. But how do I actually do it? What helps me find real joy in real suffering?

Embracing the Cross

*I*n my thoughts and prayers I am especially mindful of the many priests and religious in the Middle East who are currently experiencing a particular call to conform their lives to the mystery of the Lord's Cross. Through the difficulties facing their communities as a result of the conflicts and tensions of the region, many families are taking the decision to move away, and it can be tempting for their pastors to do likewise. In situations of this kind, though, a priest, a religious community, a parish that remains steadfast and continues to bear witness to Christ is an extraordinary sign of hope, not only for the Christians but also for all who live in the region. Their presence alone is an eloquent expression of the Gospel of peace, the determination of the Good Shepherd to care for all the sheep, the Church's unyielding commitment to dialogue, reconciliation, and loving acceptance of the other. By embracing the Cross that is held out to them, the priests and religious of the Middle East can truly radiate the hope that lies at the heart of the mystery we are celebrating in our liturgy today.

— Homily, Holy Mass Attended by Priests, Religious, Deacons, Catechists and Representatives of Cyprian Ecclesial Movements, June 5, 2010

To think about: What difficulties do I face where I am right now? What can I do to embrace those difficulties as my cross and be a sign of hope to the community?

TAKING ON THE LORD'S YOKE

*T*he traditional prayer when one puts on the *chasuble* sees it as representing the yoke of the Lord that is imposed upon us as priests. And it recalls the words of Jesus, who invites us to take his yoke upon us and to learn from him who is "gentle and lowly in heart" (*Mt* 11:29).

Taking the Lord's yoke upon us means first of all: learning from him. It means always being ready to go to his school. From him we must learn gentleness and meekness: the humility of God who shows himself in his being a man.

St. Gregory of Nazianzus once asked himself why God wanted to become a man. For me the most moving part of his answer is: "God wanted to realize what obedience means to us, and he wanted to measure everything on the basis of his own suffering. In this way, he himself can directly know what it is that we feel — what is asked of us, what indulgence we deserve — calculating our weakness on the basis of his suffering"

At times we would like to say to Jesus: Lord, your yoke is far from light. Indeed, it is tremendously heavy. But then looking at the One who bore everything — who tried out on himself obedience, weakness, suffering, all the darkness — then these complaints fade. His yoke is that of loving with him. And the more we love him and with him become loving people, the lighter becomes his seemingly burdensome yoke.

— Homily, Chrism Mass, St. Peter's Basilica, April 5, 2007

TO THINK ABOUT: How heavy does the Lord's yoke seem to me right now? How can I work on loving others more, so that the yoke will seem lighter?

PASSION INTO PRAYER

*T*o gaze upon Christ": let us look briefly now at the Crucified One above the high altar. God saved the world not by the sword, but by the Cross. In dying, Jesus extends his arms. This, in the first place, is the posture of the Passion, in which he lets himself be nailed to the Cross for us, in order to give us his life. Yet outstretched arms are also the posture of one who prays, the stance assumed by the priest when he extends his arms in prayer: Jesus transformed the Passion, his suffering and his death, into prayer, and in this way he transformed it into an act of love for God and for humanity. That, finally, is why the outstretched arms of the Crucified One are also a gesture of embracing, by which he draws us to himself, wishing to enfold us in his loving hands. In this way he is an image of the living God, he is God himself, and we may entrust ourselves to him.

— *Homily, Holy Mass on the 850th Anniversary of the Foundation of the Shrine of Mariazell, Austria, September 8. 2007*

To think about: Do my own sufferings lead me into deeper and stronger prayer? Or do I let them interfere with my prayer?

Bring the passion of this world to God

"In the days of his flesh, Jesus offered up prayers and supplications, with loud cries and tears, to him who was able to save him from death, and he was heard for his godly fear" (*Heb* 5:7). For the Letter to the Hebrews, the essential element of our being human is being compassionate, suffering with others: this is true humanity. True humanity is real participation in the suffering of human beings. It means being at the core of human passion, really bearing with others the burden of their suffering.

Here it is implied that the priest enter, like Christ, into human wretchedness, carry it with him, visit those who are suffering and look after them and, not only outwardly but also inwardly, take upon himself, recapitulate in himself the "passion" of his time, of his parish, of the people entrusted to his care. This is how Christ showed his true humanity. Of course, his Heart was always fixed on God, he always saw God, he was always in intimate conversation with him. Yet at the same time he bore the whole being, the whole of human suffering entered the Passion. In speaking, in seeing people who were lowly, who had no pastor, he suffered with them. Moreover, we priests cannot withdraw to an *Elysium*. Let us rather be immersed in the passion of this world. And with Christ's help and in communion with him, we must seek to transform it, to bring it to God.

— *Meeting with the Parish Priests of the Diocese of Rome,*
Hall of Blessings, February 18, 2010

To think about: When I feel the suffering of the world, what do I do to transform that passion — both for others and for myself — and bring it to God?

Ordained by suffering

*J*esus did not offer God some thing. Rather, he offered himself and made this offering with the very compassion that transforms the suffering of the world into a cry to the Father. Nor, in this sense, is our own priesthood limited to the religious act of Holy Mass but all of our compassion to the suffering of this world so remote from God is a priestly act. So we must learn how to accept more profoundly the sufferings of pastoral life, because priestly action is exactly this, it is mediation, it is entering into the mystery of Christ.

A second term in this context is important. It is said that by means of this obedience Christ is made perfect, in Greek *teleiothèis* (cf. *Heb* 5:8-9). The word *tèleion*, used here, means priestly ordination. Thus the Letter to the Hebrews tells us that by doing this Jesus was made a priest, and his priesthood was fulfilled. Our sacramental priestly ordination should be brought about and achieved existentially but also Christologically, and through this, should bring the world with Christ and to Christ and, with Christ, to God: thus we really become priests, *teleiothèis*. Therefore the priest is not a thing for a few hours but is fulfilled precisely in pastoral life, in his sufferings and his weaknesses, in his sorrows and also in his joys, of course. In this way we increasingly become priests in communion with Christ.

— *Meeting with the Parish Priests of the Diocese of Rome,*
Hall of Blessings, February 18, 2010

To think about: How do my sorrows and difficulties lead me closer to Christ? Or do I sometimes allow them to lead me away from Christ, into resentments and self-pity?

LOSE YOURSELF IN CHRIST

Jesus speaks of the proclamation of the Kingdom of God as the true purpose of his coming into the world. At the same time it includes his action: the signs and miracles that he works show that the Kingdom comes into the world as a present reality that ultimately coincides with Jesus himself. Christian preaching does not proclaim "words," but the Word, and the proclamation coincides with the very Person of Christ, ontologically open to the relationship with the Father and obedient to his will. Thus, an authentic service to the Word requires of the priest that he strive for deeper self-denial, to the point that he can say, with the Apostle, "it is no longer I who live, but Christ who lives in me." The priest He is not the Word but he is the "voice" of the Word.

For the priest being the "voice" of the Word implies a substantial "losing of himself" in Christ, participating with his whole being in the mystery of Christ's death and Resurrection: his understanding, his freedom, his will, and the offering of his body as a living sacrifice (cf. *Rm* 12:1-2). Only participation in Christ's sacrifice, in his kenosis, makes preaching authentic! And this is the way he must take with Christ to reach the point of being able to say to the Father, together with Christ: let "not what I will, but what you will" be done (*Mk* 14:36). Proclamation, therefore, always involves self-sacrifice, a prerequisite for its authenticity and efficacy.

— *General Audience, St. Peter's Square, June 24, 2009*

TO THINK ABOUT: How much of myself have I been willing to lose in Christ? How much am I still desperately clinging to? What worldly things stand between me and my own participation in Christ's emptying out of himself?

EIGHT

LIVING IN
THE
WORLD

The priest represents an institution that goes back to Creation. But he also lives in the modern world, with its bustle and technology.

Do we ignore all that? Or just tolerate it?

Neither, says the Holy Father: we need to embrace it. Just as the apostles used all the conveniences the Roman Empire had to offer when they set out to spread the Gospel, we need to know how to use the Internet, social media, and everything else the world gives us.

Modern technology is a challenge, but also an incalculably great opportunity. The priest's job is to use these technological wonders for the sake of the Gospel, and to not let the technology use him. The radical and revolutionary message of Christ doesn't change, even when technology does.

The priest needs to know everything about the lives of the people around him — what they do, what they care about, what they need and don't have. At the same time, he has to be recognizably a priest. In the bustle of the world, people need priests to remind them that there is something more, to pull them up out of their worldly concerns and point the way to heaven.

BE CLOSE TO THE DAILY CONCERNS OF PEOPLE'S LIVES

*T*he priest cannot be distant from the daily concerns of the People of God; on the contrary he must be very close but always with a view to salvation and of the Kingdom of God. He is the witness and steward of a life different from earthly life .He is the herald of the hope of Christ, by virtue of which we can face the present even though it may often be arduous. It is essential for the Church that the priest's identity be safeguarded with its "vertical" dimension. The lives and personality of St. John Mary Vianney and of all the Saints of your land, such as St. Hannibal Mary di Francia, are a particularly enlightening and vigorous demonstration of this.

The Church of Palermo recently commemorated the anniversary of the barbarous assassination of Fr. Giuseppe Puglisi, who belonged to this presbyterate, killed by the Mafia. His heart was on fire with authentic pastoral charity; in his zealous ministry he made a lot of room for the education of children and young people and at the same time strove to ensure that every Christian family might live its fundamental vocation as the first teacher of the faith to children. The same people entrusted to his pastoral care were able to quench their thirst with the spiritual riches of this good pastor, the cause of whose Beatification is under way. I urge you to keep alive the memory of his fruitful priestly witness, following his heroic example.

— *Address, Meeting with Bishops, Priests, Men and Women Religious, and Seminarians, Palermo, October 3, 2010*

To think about: How close am I to the daily concerns of the people around me? Do they find that trustworthy hope in me that they need from a priest in their midst?

BE THE SOUL OF THE INTERNET

*U*sing new communication technologies, priests can introduce people to the life of the Church and help our contemporaries to discover the face of Christ. They will best achieve this aim if they learn, from the time of their formation, how to use these technologies in a competent and appropriate way, shaped by sound theological insights and reflecting a strong priestly spirituality grounded in constant dialogue with the Lord. Yet priests present in the world of digital communications should be less notable for their media savvy than for their priestly heart, their closeness to Christ. This will not only enliven their pastoral outreach, but also will give a "soul" to the fabric of communications that makes up the "Web."

— *Message for the 44th World Communications Day, May 16, 2010*

TO THINK ABOUT: How do I make use of the Internet and other communications media? Do people who meet me in cyberspace see the face of Christ?

OVERTURNING THE WORLD'S VALUES

*J*esus summed up all these multiple aspects of his Priesthood in a single sentence: "The Son of Man also came not to be served but to serve, and to give his life as a ransom for many" (*Mk* 10:45).

Serving, and in so doing giving oneself; existing not for oneself but for others, on behalf of God and in view of God: this is the innermost core of Jesus Christ's mission and at the same time the true essence of his Priesthood. Thus he made the term "servant" his highest title of honor. He brought about with it an overturning of values, he gave us a new image of God and of man. Jesus does not come in the guise of a master of this world but the One who is the true Master comes as a servant. His Priesthood is not dominion but service: this is the new Priesthood of Jesus Christ, in keeping with Melchizedek.

— *Homily, Mass for the Episcopal Ordination of Five New Bishops,*
Vatican Basilica, September 12, 2009

TO THINK ABOUT: Do I really see "servant" as the highest title of honor? Or do I secretly bristle at having to do some kinds of work that strike me as undignified?

You are the man of the future

*T*he priest is the man of the future: it is he who has taken seriously Paul's words: "If then you have been raised with Christ, seek the things that are above" (*Col* 3:1). What he does on earth is in the order of the means ordered to the last things. The Mass is this one point of union between the means and the End because it already enables us to contemplate, under the humble appearances of bread and wine, the Body and Blood of the One we shall adore for eternity. "The happiness that exists in saying Mass," wrote St. John Vianney, "will only be properly understood in Heaven."

I therefore encourage you to strengthen your faith and that of your faithful in the sacrament you celebrate, which is the source of true joy. The Saint of Ars wrote: "The priest must feel the same joy (as the Apostles) in seeing Our Lord whom he holds in his hands." In giving thanks for what you are and for what you do, I repeat to you: "Nothing will ever replace the ministry of priests at the heart of the Church" (*Homily, Mass on the Esplanade des Invalides,* Paris, September 13, 2008). Living witnesses of the power of God at work in human weakness, consecrated for the salvation of the world, you remain, my dear brothers, chosen by Christ himself in order to be, through him, salt of the earth and light of the world.

— Video Message to Participants in the International Retreat for Priests,
Ars, September 27 to October 3, 2009

To think about: Are my eyes always on the future, even when the business of the present seems to overwhelm me? Does the knowledge of what the future holds help that business seem less overwhelming?

KNOW THE PERSON, NOT JUST THE ROLE

*W*ho knows the men and women of today better than the parish priest? The rectory is not in the world; rather it is in the parish. And people often come here to the parish priest, usually openly, with no pretext other than suffering, sickness, death or family matters. And they come to the confessional stripped of any veneer, with their very being. No other "profession," it seems to me, gives this possibility of knowing the person as he is, in his humanity, rather than in the role he plays in society. In this sense, we can truly study the person in his core, beyond roles, and teach ourselves what it is to be human, what it is to be in the school of Christ. To this end, it is absolutely important to come to understand the human being, the human being of today, in ourselves and with others, but also always listening attentively to the Lord and accepting in myself the seed of the word, so that it may become leaven within me and become communicable to others.

— *Address, Meeting with the Parish Priests and Clergy of the Diocese of Rome, Hall of Blessings, February 26, 2009*

TO THINK ABOUT: Do I sometimes find myself making assumptions about people according to their jobs, their race, their status, or their sex? What can I do to erase the slate and accept those people as themselves?

Only conversion leads to justice

*J*ustice cannot be created in the world solely through good economic models. Justice is achieved only if there are upright people. And there cannot be just people without the humble, daily work of conversion of hearts. This is the only way to extend corrective justice. For this reason the work of the parish priest is so fundamental, not only for the parish but also for humanity, for if there are no upright people justice will remain theoretical. Good structures cannot be established if they are opposed by people's selfishness.

This work of ours is fundamental if we are to achieve the great goals of humanity. We must work together at all levels. The universal Church must denounce, but also suggest what might be done and how it can be done. Bishops' Conferences and individual Bishops must act. And everyone must teach justice. I think that still today Abraham's dialogue with God is true and realistic (*Gn* 18:22-33), when Abraham says will you indeed destroy the city? Perhaps there are fifty righteous people, perhaps ten? And ten of the righteous are enough to ensure the city's survival. Now, if ten righteous people are lacking, notwithstanding all the economic teaching, society will not survive. Therefore we must do what is necessary to educate and to provide at least ten just people, but if possible far more. And it is precisely through our evangelization that we ensure that there are numerous righteous people and that justice may be present in the world.

— *Address, Meeting with the Parish Priests and Clergy of the Diocese of Rome, Hall of Blessings, February 26, 2009*

To think about: How do I teach justice, both in what I say and in what I do? Does what I say match what I do?

THE PRIEST MUST KEEP THE WORLD AWAKE
FOR GOD

*D*uring Lent the hymn that introduces the Office of Readings of the Liturgy of the Hours — the Office that monks once recited during the night vigil before God and for humanity — one of the duties of Lent is described with the imperative: *arctius perstemus in custodia* — we must be even more intensely alert. In the tradition of Syrian monasticism, monks were qualified as "those who remained standing." This standing was an expression of vigilance. What was considered here as a duty of the monks, we can rightly see also as an expression of the priestly mission and as a correct interpretation of the word of Deuteronomy: the priest must be on the watch. He must be on his guard in the face of the imminent powers of evil.

He must keep the world awake for God. He must be the one who remains standing: upright before the trends of time. Upright in truth. Upright in the commitment for good. Being before the Lord must always also include, at its depths, responsibility for humanity to the Lord, who in his turn takes on the burden of all of us to the Father. And it must be a taking on of him, of Christ, of his word, his truth, his love. The priest must be upright, fearless, and prepared to sustain even offenses for the Lord, as referred to in the *Acts of the Apostles*: they were "rejoicing that they were counted worthy to suffer dishonor for the name" (5:41) of Jesus.

— *Homily, Chrism Mass in St. Peter's Basilica, March 20, 2008*

TO THINK ABOUT: In my own ministry, what do I most need to be on guard against? What evil is lurking nearby?

NINE

DEALING WITH SCANDAL

Nothing is more heartbreaking than to be distrusted precisely because you're a priest. A news story appears on the television — one priest out of hundreds in your diocese, or perhaps in a diocese on the other side of the earth, has abused his position — and suddenly the world treats you like a criminal.

The world will seize on any excuse to vilify priests. And there will always be some who give the world an excuse. The wheat and the tares grow up together; priests are men, and men are sinners.

But how do we show the world that the priesthood is still holy?

Faced with exaggerations, rumors, and calumnies, Pope Benedict recommends candor and contrition — but also celebration.

Yes, there have been sinners in the priesthood. Worse, the Church has not always responded well to the problems. We can't pretend nothing bad has ever happened. We need to do what we can to make the victims whole, and to prevent more abuse from happening. More than that, we need to set a public example of repentance.

But the priesthood is still holy. The repentance should go along with a profound gratitude to God for his grace. We may be ashamed of the *actions* of certain priests, and we should be ashamed. But the world needs to see that priests are not ashamed to be priests. The very presence of sin even in the priesthood is the surest sign that the priesthood is needed, now more than ever.

Above all, every priest should work to model the ideal of priestly service, both for his parish and for the world outside. The world has a warped idea of the priesthood: it's up to Christ's priests to show the world what a priest really is.

FACE SCANDAL WITH FRANKNESS, BUT REJOICE IN GOD'S GIFT

*T*here are also, sad to say, situations that can never be sufficiently deplored where the Church herself suffers as a consequence of infidelity on the part of some of her ministers. Then it is the world that finds grounds for scandal and rejection. What is most helpful to the Church in such cases is not only a frank and complete acknowledgment of the weaknesses of her ministers, but also a joyful and renewed realization of the greatness of God's gift, embodied in the splendid example of generous pastors, religious afire with love for God and for souls, and insightful, patient spiritual guides. Here the teaching and example of Saint John Mary Vianney can serve as a significant point of reference for us all. The Curé of Ars was very humble, yet as a priest he was conscious of being an immense gift to his people: "A good shepherd, a pastor after God's heart, is the greatest treasure that the good Lord can grant to a parish, and one of the most precious gifts of divine mercy."

— *Letter Proclaiming a "Year for Priests," June 16, 2009*

TO THINK ABOUT: How can I convey the greatness of the priesthood to a world that seems to be interested in nothing but scandal?

SOME THINGS ARE ALWAYS BAD

*W*ill *Your Holiness speak about sexual abuse, and will you offer an apology?*

The Holy Father: Yes, it is essential for the Church to reconcile, to prevent, to help, and also to see guilt in these problems. We have three dimensions to clarify: the first is our moral teaching. It must be clear, it was always clear from the first centuries that priesthood is incompatible with this behavior, because the priest is in the service of Our Lord, and Our Lord is holiness in person. We have to reflect on what was insufficient in our education in recent decades: there was, in the 50s, 60s, and 70s, the idea of proportionalism in ethics: it held that nothing is bad in itself, but only in proportion to others. Now, it must be stated clearly, this was never Catholic doctrine. There are things that are always bad, and pedophilia is always bad. In our permanent formation of the priests, we have to help priests to be helpers, and not adversaries of our fellow human beings. So, we will do everything possible to clarify the teaching of the Church and help and in the preparation of priests. And we will do all possible to heal and to reconcile the victims. This is the essential content of what the word "apologize" says. It is more important to say what was insufficient in our behavior, what we must do in this moment, how we can prevent and how we all can heal and reconcile.

— Interview During the Flight to Australia, July 12, 2008

To think about: How do ideas of "proportionalism" affect the way I think about my own sins? Am I tempted to dismiss some of my transgressions — dishonesty, for example, or anger — because they seem proportionally harmless?

DEALING WITH ABUSE

The sexual abuse scandals have shaken the trust of the faithful in the Church. How do you intend to act so as to re-establish this trust?

The Holy Father: Above all I must say that these revelations were a shock for me. They are a great sadness, and it is hard to understand how this perversion of the priestly ministry was possible. It is a great sadness also that Church leadership was not sufficiently vigilant and sufficiently swift and decisive in taking the necessary measures. On account of this we are living a time of penance, humility, renewed sincerity, as I wrote to the Irish Bishops. I feel that we must now be engaged in a time of penance, a time of humility; we must renew and learn again absolute sincerity. In relation to the victims I would like to say that there are three important things. Our first interest must be the victims; how to repair the damage, how to assist these persons in overcoming their trauma, in finding life again, in finding again trust in the message of Christ. Secondly there is the problem of those who are guilty. A just penalty must exclude them from all access to young people. Thirdly there is the question of prevention through education and the selection of candidates to the priesthood. We must be in such a way attentive so as to exclude, according to human possibilities, future cases.

— *Interview with Journalists During the Flight to the United Kingdom,*
September 10, 2010

To **THINK ABOUT:** What can I be doing right now to assist the victims of abuse in the Church?

ACKNOWLEDGE OUR SINS

*I*t is true that the problem of child abuse is peculiar neither to Ireland nor to the Church. Nevertheless, the task you now face is to address the problem of abuse that has occurred within the Irish Catholic community, and to do so with courage and determination. No one imagines that this painful situation will be resolved swiftly. Real progress has been made, yet much more remains to be done. Perseverance and prayer are needed, with great trust in the healing power of God's grace.

At the same time, I must also express my conviction that, in order to recover from this grievous wound, the Church in Ireland must first acknowledge before the Lord and before others the serious sins committed against defenseless children. Such an acknowledgement, accompanied by sincere sorrow for the damage caused to these victims and their families, must lead to a concerted effort to ensure the protection of children from similar crimes in the future.

As you take up the challenges of this hour, I ask you to remember "the rock from which you were hewn" (*Is* 51:1). Reflect upon the generous, often heroic, contributions made by past generations of Irish men and women to the Church and to humanity as a whole, and let this provide the impetus for honest self-examination and a committed program of ecclesial and individual renewal. It is my prayer that, assisted by the intercession of her many saints, and purified through penance, the Church in Ireland will overcome the present crisis.

— *Pastoral Letter to the Catholics of Ireland, March 19, 2010*

To think about: How do I acknowledge the sins that have been committed in the Church, even when I'm not guilty of them? And how do I do it without seeming to forget the truth that the Church is still a divine institution, in spite of its fallen and sinful members?

RESPOND WITH PRAYER

To the priests and religious of Ireland:
All of us are suffering as a result of the sins of our confreres who betrayed a sacred trust or failed to deal justly and responsibly with allegations of abuse. In view of the outrage and indignation that this has provoked many of you feel personally discouraged, even abandoned In some people's eyes you are tainted by association, and viewed as if you were somehow responsible for the misdeeds of others. At this painful time, I want to acknowledge the dedication of your priestly and religious lives and apostolates, and I invite you to reaffirm your faith in Christ, your love of his Church, and your confidence in the Gospel's promise of redemption, forgiveness, and interior renewal. In this way, you will demonstrate for all to see that where sin abounds, grace abounds all the more (cf. *Rom* 5:20).

I know that many of you are disappointed, bewildered, and angered by the way these matters have been handled by some of your superiors. Yet, it is essential that you cooperate closely with those in authority and help to ensure that the measures adopted to respond to the crisis will be truly evangelical, just, and effective. Above all, I urge you to become ever more clearly men and women of prayer, courageously following the path of conversion, purification, and reconciliation. In this way, the Church in Ireland will draw new life and vitality from your witness to the Lord's redeeming power made visible in your lives.

— *Pastoral Letter to the Catholics of Ireland, March 19, 2010*

To think about: When people seem to treat me as guilty of heinous sins merely by being a priest, do I respond with rage or with prayer? Do I remember to pray especially for those who misunderstand the priesthood so completely that they think it a virtue to insult priests?

Do not despair of God's mercy

To priests and religious who have abused children:

You betrayed the trust that was placed in you by innocent young people and their parents, and you must answer for it before Almighty God and before properly constituted tribunals. You have forfeited the esteem of the people of Ireland and brought shame and dishonor upon your confrères. Those of you who are priests violated the sanctity of the sacrament of Holy Orders in which Christ makes himself present in us and in our actions. Together with the immense harm done to victims, great damage has been done to the Church and to the public perception of the priesthood and religious life.

I urge you to examine your conscience, take responsibility for the sins you have committed, and humbly express your sorrow. Sincere repentance opens the door to God's forgiveness and the grace of true amendment. By offering prayers and penances for those you have wronged, you should seek to atone personally for your actions. Christ's redeeming sacrifice has the power to forgive even the gravest of sins, and to bring forth good from even the most terrible evil. At the same time, God's justice summons us to give an account of our actions and to conceal nothing. Openly acknowledge your guilt, submit yourselves to the demands of justice, but do not despair of God's mercy.

— *Pastoral Letter to the Catholics of Ireland, March 19, 2010*

TO THINK ABOUT: Though I may never have done serious harm to anyone in my care, what subtler violations of my vows am I guilty of? Are there unrepented sins of pride, or wrath, or sloth weighing on my conscience?

MORE IMPORTANT TO HAVE GOOD PRIESTS THAN MANY PRIESTS

The American People are expecting a message from you on this crisis. What will be your message for this suffering Church?

The Holy Father: It is a great suffering for the Church in the United States and for the Church in general, for me personally, that this could happen. It is difficult for me to understand how it was possible for priests to fail in this way. I am ashamed, and we will do everything possible to ensure that this does not happen in future. We have to act on three levels: the first is at the level of justice and the political level. We will absolutely exclude pedophiles from the sacred ministry.... So at this first level we can do justice and help the victims, because they are deeply affected. Then there is a pastoral level. The victims will need healing and help and assistance and reconciliation: this is a big pastoral engagement, and I know that the bishops and the priests and all Catholic people in the United States will do whatever possible to help, to assist, to heal. We will do all that is possible in the education of seminarians for a deep spiritual, human, and intellectual formation for the students. So, I know that the bishops and directors of seminarians will do all possible to have a strong, strong discernment because it is more important to have good priests than to have many priests. This is also our third level.

— *Interview During the Flight to the United States of America,
April 15, 2008*

To think about: What could I be doing to heal the wounds in our Church? How does my own life show the world a counter-example of the holiness of the priesthood?

A Prayer for Priests

Immaculate Mother,
in this place of grace,
called together by the love of your Son Jesus
the Eternal High Priest, we,
sons in the Son and his priests,
consecrate ourselves to your maternal Heart,
in order to carry out faithfully the Father's Will.

We are mindful that, without Jesus,
we can do nothing good (cf. *Jn* 15:5)
and that only through him, with him, and in him,
will we be instruments of salvation
for the world.

Bride of the Holy Spirit,
obtain for us the inestimable gift
of transformation in Christ.
Through the same power of the Spirit that
overshadowed you,
making you the Mother of the Savior,
help us to bring Christ your Son
to birth in ourselves too.
May the Church
be thus renewed by priests who are holy,
priests transfigured by the grace of him
who makes all things new.

Mother of Mercy,
it was your Son Jesus who called us
to become like him:
light of the world and salt of the earth
(cf. *Mt* 5:13-14).

Help us,
through your powerful intercession,
never to fall short of this sublime vocation,
nor to give way to our selfishness,
to the allurements of the world
and to the wiles of the Evil One.

Preserve us with your purity,
guard us with your humility
and enfold us with your maternal love
that is reflected in so many souls
consecrated to you,
who have become for us
true spiritual mothers.

Mother of the Church,
we priests want to be pastors
who do not feed themselves
but rather give themselves to God for their brethren,
finding their happiness in this.
Not only with words, but with our lives,
we want to repeat humbly,

day after day,
Our "here I am."

Guided by you,
we want to be Apostles
of Divine Mercy,
glad to celebrate every day
the Holy Sacrifice of the Altar
and to offer to those who request it
the sacrament of Reconciliation.

Repeat to the Lord
your efficacious word:
"They have no wine" (*Jn* 2:3),
so that the Father and the Son will send upon us
a new outpouring of
the Holy Spirit.
Full of wonder and gratitude
at your continuing presence in our midst,
in the name of all priests
I too want to cry out:
"Why is this granted me,
that the mother of my Lord should come to me?" (*Lk* 1:43).

Our Mother for all time,
do not tire of "visiting us,"
consoling us, sustaining us.
Come to our aid

and deliver us from every danger
that threatens us.
With this act of entrustment and consecration,
we wish to welcome you
more deeply, more radically,
for ever and totally
into our human and priestly lives.

Let your presence cause new blooms to burst forth
in the desert of our loneliness,
let it cause the sun to shine on our darkness,
let it restore calm after the tempest,
so that all mankind shall see the salvation
of the Lord,
who has the name and the face of Jesus,
who is reflected in our hearts,
for ever united to yours!

Amen!

— Prayer, Act of Entrustment and Consecration of Priests
to the Immaculate Heart of Mary, May 12, 2010

SOURCES

One / It Does Make Sense

Page 13 — www.vatican.va/holy_father/benedict_xvi/letters/2010/documents/
hf_ben-xvi_let_20101018_seminaristi_en.html

Page 14 — www.vatican.va/holy_father/benedict_xvi/speeches/2006/april/
documents/hf_ben-xvi_spe_20060406_xxi-wyd_en.html

Page 15 — www.vatican.va/holy_father/benedict_xvi/audiences/2009/
documents/hf_ben-xvi_aud_20090819_en.html

Page 16 — www.vatican.va/holy_father/benedict_xvi/homilies/2008/
documents/hf_ben-xvi_hom_20080427_ordinazioni-sacerdotali_en.html

Page 17 — www.vatican.va/holy_father/benedict_xvi/speeches/2009/june/
documents/hf_ben-xvi_spe_20090606_seminaire_en.html

Page 18 — www.vatican.va/holy_father/benedict_xvi/speeches/2008/april/
documents/hf_ben-xvi_spe_20080419_st-joseph-seminary_en.html

Page 19 — www.vatican.va/holy_father/benedict_xvi/messages/youth/
documents/hf_ben-xvi_mes_20100806_youth_en.html

Page 20 — www.vatican.va/holy_father/benedict_xvi/messages/youth/
documents/hf_ben-xvi_mes_20100222_youth_en.html

Page 21 — www.vatican.va/holy_father/benedict_xvi/speeches/2005/august/
documents/hf_ben-xvi_spe_20050819_seminarians_en.html

Page 22 — www.vatican.va/holy_father/benedict_xvi/speeches/2005/august/
documents/hf_ben-xvi_spe_20050819_seminarians_en.html

Page 23 — www.vatican.va/holy_father/benedict_xvi/speeches/2005/august/
documents/hf_ben-xvi_spe_20050819_seminarians_en.html

Page 24 — www.vatican.va/holy_father/benedict_xvi/speeches/2005/august/
documents/hf_ben-xvi_spe_20050819_seminarians_en.html

Page 25 — www.vatican.va/holy_father/benedict_xvi/speeches/2005/august/
documents/hf_ben-xvi_spe_20050819_seminarians_en.html

Page 26 — www.vatican.va/holy_father/benedict_xvi/speeches/2010/october/
documents/hf_ben-xvi_spe_20101003_palermo-cattedrale_en.html

Page 27— www.vatican.va/holy_father/benedict_xvi/homilies/2008/
documents/hf_ben-xvi_hom_20080913_parigi-esplanade_en.html

Two / A Bridge to God

Page 30 — www.vatican.va/holy_father/benedict_xvi/audiences/2010/
documents/hf_ben-xvi_aud_20100505_en.html

Page 31— www.vatican.va/holy_father/benedict_xvi/homilies/2010/
documents/hf_ben-xvi_hom_20100611_concl-anno-sac_en.html

Page 32— www.vatican.va/holy_father/benedict_xvi/audiences/2010/
documents/hf_ben-xvi_aud_20100505_en.html

Page 33 — www.vatican.va/holy_father/benedict_xvi/homilies/2009/
documents/hf_ben-xvi_hom_20090611_corpus-domini_en.html

Page 34 — www.vatican.va/holy_father/benedict_xvi/apost_exhortations/
documents/hf_ben-xvi_exh_20070222_sacramentum-caritatis_en.html

Page 35 — www.vatican.va/holy_father/benedict_xvi/apost_exhortations/
documents/hf_ben-xvi_exh_20070222_sacramentum-caritatis_en.html

Page 36— www.vatican.va/holy_father/benedict_xvi/speeches/2005/may/
documents/hf_ben-xvi_spe_20050513_roman-clergy_en.html

Page 37— www.vatican.va/holy_father/benedict_xvi/homilies/2008/
documents/hf_ben-xvi_hom_20080622_quebec_en.html

Three / The Priority of Prayer

Four / Living in the Body of Christ

Page 66 — www.vatican.va/holy_father/benedict_xvi/speeches/2006/
september/documents/hf_ben-xvi_spe_20060914_clergy-freising_en.html

Page 67 — www.vatican.va/holy_father/benedict_xvi/homilies/2008/
documents/hf_ben-xvi_hom_20080427_ordinazioni-sacerdotali_en.html

Page 68 — www.vatican.va/holy_father/benedict_xvi/homilies/2008/
documents/hf_ben-xvi_hom_20080622_quebec_en.html

Five / Celibacy

Page 71 — www.vatican.va/holy_father/benedict_xvi/speeches/2010/june/
documents/hf_ben-xvi_spe_20100610_concl-anno-sac_en.html

Page 72 — www.vatican.va/holy_father/benedict_xvi/speeches/2010/june/
documents/hf_ben-xvi_spe_20100610_concl-anno-sac_en.html

Page 73 — www.vatican.va/holy_father/benedict_xvi/letters/2007/documents/
hf_ben-xvi_let_20070527_china_en.html

Six / Leading by Example

Page 77 — www.vatican.va/holy_father/benedict_xvi/speeches/2006/august/
documents/hf_ben-xvi_spe_20060831_sacerdoti-albano_en.html

Page 78 — www.vatican.va/holy_father/benedict_xvi/speeches/2010/june/
documents/hf_ben-xvi_spe_20100610_concl-anno-sac_en.html

Page 79 — www.vatican.va/holy_father/benedict_xvi/speeches/2010/march/
documents/hf_ben-xvi_spe_20100311_penitenzieria_en.html

Page 80 — www.vatican.va/holy_father/benedict_xvi/speeches/2006/may/
documents/hf_ben-xvi_spe_20060525_poland-clergy_en.html

Page 81 — www.vatican.va/holy_father/benedict_xvi/homilies/2009/
documents/hf_ben-xvi_hom_20090912_ord-episcopale_en.html

Seven / Suffering

Eight / Living in the World

Nine / Dealing with Scandal

Page 110 — www.vatican.va/holy_father/benedict_xvi/speeches/2008/july/documents/hf_ben-xvi_spe_20080712_interview_en.html

Page 111 — www.vatican.va/holy_father/benedict_xvi/speeches/2010/september/documents/hf_ben-xvi_spe_20100916_interv-regno-unito_en.html

Page 112 — www.vatican.va/holy_father/benedict_xvi/letters/2010/documents/hf_ben-xvi_let_20100319_church-ireland_en.html

Page 113 — www.vatican.va/holy_father/benedict_xvi/letters/2010/documents/hf_ben-xvi_let_20100319_church-ireland_en.html

Page 114 — www.vatican.va/holy_father/benedict_xvi/letters/2010/documents/hf_ben-xvi_let_20100319_church-ireland_en.html

Page 115 — www.vatican.va/holy_father/benedict_xvi/speeches/2008/april/documents/hf_ben-xvi_spe_20080415_intervista-usa_en.html

A Prayer for Priests

Page 117 — www.vatican.va/holy_father/benedict_xvi/prayers/documents/hf_ben-xvi_20100512_affidamento-fatima_en.html